The

VP Annual

2016

The VP

Annual

2016

Verbivoracious Press

Glentrees, 13 Mt Sinai Lane, Singapore

This edition published in Great Britain & Singapore

by Verbivoracious Press

www.verbivoraciouspress.org

ISBN: 978-981-09-8486-1

Printed and bound in Great Britain & Singapore

CONTENTS

CONTENTS

VP ANNUAL 2016

Introduction

EDITORS

The verbivore emerges, prognathous and slavering, from its cocoon, having consumed four festschrifts and fifteen books, ravenous for further reading material on the exploratory and the outré. To appease its needs, we have assembled the first in a proposed series of VP Annuals, miscellanies of essay, creative non-fiction, and author interviews. Our supreme mistress, Dame Christine Brooke-Rose, is remembered in Michael Freeman's 'Amalgammemoir', a warm and revealing portrait of the author in her fractious final decade, and Stephanie Jane Jones's essay on the underrated *Next*. Among the scholarship includes Monika Fludernik's incisive criticism on Gabriel Josipovici, Douglas Field's passion for the lost fictions of Jeff Nutall, and Dana A. Williams's take on Leon Forrest. Among the creative non-fiction: VP favourite Gilbert Adair returns in James Langdon's attempt to recreate a lost interview with the late author, John Trefry constructs his own intricate pattern in homage to Jacques Roubaud, and Doug Nufer outlines the construction of his constraint-based novel *Never Again*. Our interviews for this issue include a long conversation with Steven Moore, conducted by Nicolas Tredell, encompassing the critic's early days as a novelist manqué to his iconoclastic later years, a mid-90s talk with Rikki Ducornet (conducted by Moore), and a short talk with *Darconville's Cat* author Alexander Theroux. Now, having satisfied the verbivore's appetite for another few weeks, we return to our lair to prepare for another year of stellar festschrifts, reprints, and perhaps some fresh fiction. We hope the following will satisfy your cravings.

Amalgammemoir

MICHAEL FREEMAN

The editors of the VP Annual invited me to contribute a reminiscence of Christine Brooke-Rose. The obituaries have come and gone. The literary evaluations are well under way. A Christine Brooke-Rose Society is gathering speed. Others have calibrated her distinctive literary achievement, though she was her own most astute and theoretically reflexive critic. What follows here is merely an amalgam of personal recollections and the correspondence that Christine and I shared from when I knew her first as an editor then as a friend across the years from *Amalgamemnon* [1984] to *Life, End of . . .* [2006] and her death in 2012. This compilation cheerfully presupposes a porous membrane between her work and personality, evident enough from her autobiographical novel *Remake*. Laying no claim to particular insight or overview, what follows, a bricolage, is a collateral homage to an old friend.

Although the letters I refer to were written to me, legal protocol leaves copyright with Christine's estate and I'm grateful to Jean-Michel Rabaté, her friend and executor, for permission to quote the extracts, and to Carcanet for the quotations from *Life, End of.*

Corn Exchange to Cabrières

It was George Steiner who suggested to Christine that she should send the text of *Amalgamemnon* to Carcanet Press, our office squeezed into Manchester's old Corn Exchange, where we had started adding translations of modern European fiction to our core list of poetry. I'd been appointed a fiction editor with a particular brief for 'experimental' fiction, and was already familiar with her earlier novels, so when her unsolicited typescript turned up I brandished it round the editorial office until it was agreed we should publish what became the first novel of the 'third wave' of her fiction. What I'd call the first wave were the relatively conventional novels and short stories like *The Sycamore Tree* and *Go When You See the Green Man Walking*; the second wave, the determinedly experimental series *Out, Such, Between, Thru*. The third wave—insofar as her heterogeneous novels can be yoked together—became that astonishing ensemble where technical innovation and not-so-crypto autobiographical strands interweave, each novel a new departure, and each departure finding its correlative in the academic articles that became the theory, praxis, polemic of *Invisible Author*. My quasi-editorial friendship with Christine over these years, catching up with her at our homes, at publishing events and conferences, wasn't always easy but it proved weather-proof.

Here's a typical touch of that weather. In 1987 she wrote to me from Aachen: "I'm lecturing at Warwick on 7th March, but I guess that's too far for you, then I'll be going straight back to Germany. It's a conference on philosophy and literature. But then if you [*the Carcanet editors*] didn't any of you come and listen when I was in Manchester, why should you go all the way to Warwick? [I'm teasing.]" The conference was to be held at Cris Nash's department. Christine knew his *World-Games* [1987] on the anti-realist tradition, and later thought well of his 1990 novel *The Dinosaurs Ball* [sic] which we published at Carcanet: "What Kafka did for the law and the civil service, Cristopher Nash does for medicine," as Christine offered us for the blurb. So my wife drove us through foul weather to the conference where we burst in late and snow-covered just as Christine was delivering her paper, dressed in Parisian *chic* and her hard-travellin' trainers. From Aachen a month later "I meant to write sooner to thank you both for driving all that way in the snow to hear me—just because of a tease! I do hope you got back all right, the radio that night said everything was blocked in the Pennines. Anyway, I appreciated it and it was lovely to see you both again."

So it went, but basically our relationship might be tracked by her inscriptions in my copy of *Amalgamemnon* [1984] and of *Life, End of . .* [2006]: first "For Mike, in anticipation of a splendid collaboration . . ." then "For Jennifer and Mike, with gratitude and love . . ." At least she didn't see us as mere fair-weather friends.

Whatever the weather, you couldn't get anything past her. With her kitbag of erudition, stern logic, unpredictable wit, street-fighting polemic, fierce intelligence and unpredictable imagination, she always kept you guessing and often left you bemused. Occasionally you simply had to duck and cover in your fox-hole until the shrapnel eased off. There was something of a CB-R carapace with a few chips on its surface but tucked inside was a warmth and sheer kindliness that survived the problems and her disappointments of later years.

"Odds and ends and new beginnings"

That was how she headed a long e-mail in June 2002. Touching so many of her preoccupations at the time and revealing a self-reflective vulnerability it remains a key-note in my memories of Christine. We'd been talking of age and loneliness, and she responded that she had "so managed things as to be alone-in-the-world [which I love] . . . I'm learning serenity [in fact, I'm a naturally happy person], it's just that I didn't expect other people to behave the way they do and the way I probably behaved unwittingly, but it was pretty naïve of me not to. Since reading the entire war day by day from the enemy viewpoint I am more conscious of this [*people's sheer otherness*] than most people and quick to apologise . . . After all, imagining the other ties up with the teaching problem we exchanged views on in our previous letters: a good teacher must learn to re-imagine his/her ignorance. I came to teaching late [at 45] and had to learn this lesson quickly, but was infinitely helped by being thrown into Structuralism and Post-Structuralism at the same time and having to teach both for different levels, learning as I went! And even now I'm haunted by a book I shall never write [no more energy] called 'The Art of Unlearning', going Kundera-like in and out of fiction [eg. Trollope's 'He Knew He Was Right', rather like Kundera's Goethe in 'Immortality' but also [broadly] about peace in the world if only people could unlearn the legends and dogmas they're willing to kill and die for."

The Invisible Author

For Christine, authorial invisibility meant two things. One was a matter of story-telling, strategies which she explicated in her theoretical essays, though as a more qualified and nuanced position than the totalising assertions of the Barthes cadre. The other was a matter of regret: that she didn't get the notice she deserved. A few discerning critics—like Frank Kermode and Lorna Sage—saw what she was about and gave her credit, but she came to feel—though she was ahead of the game—she was a prophet without honour in her own country, and in other countries was assimilated too blandly into their own traditions of experiment, despite her refusal to be plugged into *nouveau roman* stereotypes. And she resisted suggestions of British parallels: "I was surprised Kermode thought so highly of BSJ *[Johnson]* . . . though I imagine he *[Kermode]* would be the first to say that the supposed experiments have nothing to do with the content. Just added bits. I have struggled so hard to invent things that become one with the content . . . " [2004].

She acknowledged that she hadn't helped her status or sales by opting for self-exile, but didn't feel that the promotion circuit should have been so necessary. Even Carcanet Press, her only fiction publisher from *Amalgamemnon* onwards, didn't—perhaps we couldn't—live up to her expectations in promotion or editorial attentiveness, and I sometimes suspected that we had become her publisher *faute de mieux*. Writing from her walled-in house in Cabrières d'Avignon, and feeling rather walled-out again, she told me that her essays in *Invisible Author* were importantly for her "a sort of testament" but that her usual academic publisher had turned it down on synopsis only, "and I was too fatigued even to send parcels around, so I let a friend and fan from Irvine take it away and send it to Ohio. That's how much I'm appreciated in my own country now! But I don't mind, I've reached serenity about that too." Ohio State University Press did publish it though she grumbled that it took them two years to do so . . . "Serenity" was a mode [maybe a default mode] she often and insistently affirmed from then [2002] on. However in her final years any residual serenity was severely tested. She felt isolated from her friends; her hearing and eye-sight declined sharply; her polyneuritis—"Polly can't even put the kettle on!"—eventually brought her to near-paralysis. Phone calls in her last couple of years were bedevilled by your unsureness whether she was hallucinating, cheerfully sending you up again, or carefully setting you up as a character in her next novel as she'd done in *Life, End of*; she tended to keep her friends in separate safety-deposit boxes until the occasion—like the characterisation in the next novel—demanded some interface. I hesitated whether to mention her final frailties, but Christine was always one for 'telling it how it is', albeit in new forms of mimesis, just as her last two novels were clearly ruminations on the author-as-narrator-as-character nexus, at the same time revealing many of her anxious preoccupations in a scarcely oblique way.

A Trinity

I'd been teasing Christine about her early *A Grammar of Metaphor* [1958], suggesting she had worked up a syntactically orientated framework parallel to Empson's typology of ambiguities, and in both cases the scaffolding mattered much less than the particular analyses. After a typically sharp rebuttal, she took the comparison as praising with faint damns, particularly when I mentioned that Empson had been my tutor at Sheffield at just the time *A Grammar of Metaphor* appeared, and he had been a kindly and scrupulously conscientious teacher as well as the acclaimed critic. "What you say of your experience of Empson is interesting. I met him much later in Hampstead, but never knew him well. For the later Structuralists, he'd have been chaos [if they'd ever heard of him, which they hadn't, Barthes thinking he'd invented 'polysémie', as I say somewhere in my new book]. Empson was the first to think creatively about form, so I'm not surprised you became such an open-minded and subtle reader." Christine knew how to flatter her friends, as well as being a street-fighting academic. Perhaps that "open-minded" concealed her thought that I didn't know enough; she knew I struggled with her theoretical expositions. Her "new book" *Invisible Author: Last Essays* came out in 2002; I'd received her letter in February of that year.

She quite liked to be teased as it gave her another cue to put you and the neglectful literary establishment to rights, especially in her self-imposed exile in Lou Jas. A few years later I reminded her—again in a tease—that she and Empson had been elevated to a holy trinity when George Steiner had cited her *A Grammar of Metaphor* along with Empson's *Seven Types of Ambiguity* and *The Structure of Complex Words* and Donald Davie's *Articulate Energy* and *Purity of Diction in English Verse* as key critical texts in the way linguistics contributes to understanding of literature. [*Conversations with Critics*, Nicolas Tredell 1994]. This prompted a phone call from her, insisting that Empson knew how language worked but was making up his linguistics as he went along, whereas she knew much more about the theory of linguistics than either he or Davie, and anyway had been a comparative linguist since her early years as a medievalist, not to mention her polyglot European upbringing. *So there!* It was only later I noticed that she had taken Davie to task in *A Grammar of Metaphor*, allowing that his study of syntax is close to hers but less concerned with metaphor than with poetic language in general, and repeatedly relies on a "conceptual approach" in his *Articulate Energy* [1955].

Later I got to know Davie at Carcanet, where I discovered that he and I shared [as well as some years in Barnsley] an admiration of Christine's criticism for not being reductivist or totalising. My own view is, straightforwardly, that what Empson did for how we read poetry so Christine did for how we read—or should read—fiction. The synoptic *Rhetoric of the Unreal*, then *Stories, Theories and Things* and *Invisible Author* between them build a theory of fiction, with an analysis of its theory and theoreticians, that constitutes an extraordinary body of work to match her own novels. Others will set out—already have—the symmetries between her novels and her theorising, what we once would have called her *praxis.* Less straightforward are some asymmetries between her genre-theorising and her autobiographic rumination as the one is increasingly refracted in the other in the later novels, though with a little retrospection the refractions were always there.

Blenheims and Bletchley

I'd mentioned to her that I was born in Stockton just before the war, across the Tees from the RAF base at Thornaby where she'd been posted three years later to Coastal Command. My anecdote of an uncle's death at a Bomber Command base at Lisset and the official cover-up of his Halifax bomber's structural fault launched Christine into a tutorial on Thornaby's work-horse aircraft, the Blenheims, Avro Ansons, and Lockheed Hudsons, their failings as reconnaissance and bombing aircraft, and the RAF's war-time myth-making. "Of course I want to read your 'anecdotage'. At my age it's become far more interesting than learned disquisitions. I remember Stockton's High Street pubs very well, that's where the Coastal Command pilot would drink and take me out, and sometimes I never saw them again. The High Street was very wide, almost like a market-place, and that's where I found a tailor to make my WAAF uniform when I got my commission at 18 before going to the OTC in Loughborough, then on to Bletchley. Where, incidentally, I was *never* an interceptor! Strange how nobody can get that right, even when they've read *Remake.* I've been called a decoder before, but never demoted to interceptor! I was an Intelligence Officer, ie I dealt with the intelligence once intercepted and decoded. But I forgive you. How can the young know what they didn't experience? [You see, I flatter you to show I forgive]." [2003]

In a letter a year later she writes "Strange to think that in 1941 I may have been walking up that wide High Street in Stockton, and passed a small boy in a latish pram whom I would meet one day at my publisher's."

[That "latish" [late-ish] must mean I'd be too old for a pram and ought to have been in a push-chair or walking, to meet her stern war-time standards?] I sent her a photograph to remind her of her stay, forty years later, in our cottage in Yorkshire, and she wrote "As for your house it sounds bigger than I remember. In my mind I see a one-up one-down and feel terrible about your lending me your only bedroom and [*you and Jennifer*] sleeping downstairs somewhere. But now I see it's double, so I can drop that particular guilt, thank you doctor." During that stay she was cautious with our Gordon Setter but welcomed the Cairn Terrier onto her lap, pleased that it was called Rosie. Of course when we took her for dinner at The Dumb Waiter in Todmorden she greeted the manager with allusions to Pinter and the "twice-dead?" place-name of the town, then delighted to see her food hauled up from the kitchen-cellar on an actual 'dumb-waiter' lift.

Poems and politics at bay

In 2003 I'd sent her some recent poetry anthologies. She writes "I didn't want them to influence my own poor prose efforts. Curiously, my favourite poem by each so far is dedicated to Heaney. Longley's 'A Personal Statement' which somehow reminded me of my own arteries etc., and Mahon's poem [can't find it again] on being various dead things through the ages . . . I'd never heard of either [poet]. The reason is that I more or less stopped reading poetry after my Pound book because I had 'found myself' in novels on the one hand, narratology on the other. Oh, I taught some poetry classes, but that was part of a liking for theory. In my twenties I would, like everyone, write at least a poem a day, all bad, but stopped after my first novel ['57]". Later in 2004 she mentioned "Haven't written a line [of poetry] since the late fifties after I discovered I wasn't a poet. I think any poetry left in me has gone into my novels and certainly in this one [*Life, End of*]".

She had a sharp eye for how a good poem works, as elaborated in her *A Grammar of Metaphor*, and would pounce on a lesser effort. *PN Review* had published a verse letter of mine to Christine but it didn't go down at all well with her, and she phoned me promptly with her pragmatic objections to the poem's allusions. How many readers can know where or even what my Lou Jas is? 'Châtelaine' will make them think I live in a grand château, not an ordinary house in the village. Who will remember that the green man walking was the title for my book of short stories decades ago? Anyway, it reads like my obituary—some *Eheu fugaces, Postume, Postume!* This, at least, was the gist from the startled notes I'd scribbled, as I did after some of her phone conversations. You never knew when she would chase you up for misremembering or misattributing a point; she'd probably pick holes all over these present recollections. I suppose she was right, as the poem ended " . . . Mira now admits / No subscripts, remakes, brooks no rosy nexts." And of course she cautiously resisted the identification with Mira of *Amalgamemnon.*

"I sometimes feel like the poet Arnaut Daniel, made to speak one of his verses in Provençal by Dante in the Purgatario, in homage to another vernacular which, however, did not survive strongly enough to become the national language of France as did Dante's Italian . . . I feel like Arnaut because he never became part of the mainstream." This letter [2003] probably reflects her growing sense that her work had been marginalised by the English literary establishment, but it was also a political response, as I'd been worrying about staying in the Labour Party, suggesting it was like a new Dantesque circle for the damned if they do and damned if they don't. She wrote "The Left seems completely scattered everywhere. In GB it has become the Right, pro-burning Bush. In France it had to vote for Chirac to prevent worse, but finds itself unable to reconstitute itself, admitting its errors and *guerre des chefs,* etc. . . . As for the 'extreme' Left [in fact reactionary] of the ex-Soviet constellation, it keeps hovering between the two systems. Only Scandinavia seems to have remained somewhere near what you and I mean by the Left without sacrificing business. . . . Here too we wait in Purgo, hoping to avoid the Inferno. That's how you should regard your present doubts. Love, Christine."

"Have you noticed Tony Blair's eyes looking more and more

hallucinated, wide open and staring? It looks as if the new Labour Party might throw him out as the Tories did to his *maîtresse à penser*." I'd been telling her about the local political frustrations that Jennifer and I were facing as we laboured in the Labour vineyard, with Jennifer taking a very active role in the Constituency Labour Party. She observed "I'm a bit worried about Jennifer. It's not a wise choice to throw oneself body and soul into anything, one is always disappointed, more especially with politicians who wouldn't be politicians unless they were stupid. It's a special job, attracting only those who can think four years ahead and no more, and enjoy intrigues etc. Can't she just relax and enjoy her own life now? Why do excellent women always need self-sacrifice?" That "now" refers to Jennifer's retirement from teaching. It's a not uncharacteristic mix of a remark: genuine concern at the personal level, and a willingness to swing wildly at the general, especially when it comes to politics.

Pedagogy and politics at bay

Mentioning my wife's irritation with government-imposed schemes and protocols in British schools, this touched a nerve about Christine's years at Vincennes, the university campus set up by the French government to dodge or divert the critique of the *soixante-huitards*. An e-mail in 2003 was headed 'Schools of stupidity': "I wasn't a teacher by profession but turned to it because my books couldn't possibly support me. But I took it very seriously, learnt the art of transmitting enthusiasm orally—there's something of an actor in every teacher, though many have forgotten that and stand like automata. Nevertheless I heaved a sigh of relief when my retirement age came. At last I could give all my time to writing."

A letter later in that year suggests reasons for her 'relief'. She thought that too many students had been inadequately taught at school and were admitted to open-entry Vincennes with a "hatred of literature". She found the "demagogic" demands for mixed-ability teaching were getting harder as the heterogeneity increased, the problems being exacerbated by the cultural and linguistic range of the multi-ethnic classes. There are hints here of a recurring dilemma for Christine in other contexts. She saw herself firmly as a principled woman of The Left but with an equally firm critique of the positions adopted by its parties and professionals. "I could never join a party, a religion, a social group, a clique—hence my troubles with Other People now that I'm alone in the world. . . . I had huge problems arriving in France into a left-wing university following the permanent rows between the CP [astonishingly alive compared with that in England] and *gauchistes,* which affected every pedagogic and other problems." [2002]

Institutional politics and ideological bedrocks, she thought, distorted the principles and actual practice of good teaching; and then "bad teachers produce more bad teachers and we get what you call 'dysfunctional' headteachers." [1999] I'd let slip that before getting into publishing I'd lectured in teacher-training, and Jennifer thought the headteacher where she taught was 'dysfunctional' and in need of re-training. When it came particularly to teaching literature Christine thought there was an endemic *trahison des clercs*: students were allowed to get away with an ignorance and imprecision that wouldn't be tolerated in courses for doctors and engineers. Not that she criticised imaginative teaching. She was intrigued to hear of Jennifer's lesson, in her primary school, on levels of 'representation'. The class had been presented with our large English Setter, a larger-than-life expressionist painting of the same dog, a discussion of the differences between the image in the frame and the actual dog in the room, and then having to do a 'portrait' of the dog in a painting or a poem. Christine was delighted at representation being problematised in a primary school, brightly referring us to her exegeses of 'representation' in her *A Rhetoric of the Unreal.* The book Christine should have added to her *oeuvre* was *The Comic and the Meta-comic in Education.*

The comedy in her novels was something she felt hadn't been appreciated. In their different forms they amounted to a radical satire of society and its ideologies, of academic institutions and their narcissism. She was a participant-observer on an expedition of cultural anthropology.

But she thought that even sympathetic readers of her novels didn't attach enough importance to the humour. I was gently told off for that too: the Joycean word-play in her work wasn't just to prise open conventional thought-packages; it was also for the sheer fun of it.

Subscript and sub-structure

Although she never subscribed to OULIPO protocols and paradigms, she often worked with firmly imposed syntactic constraints in her novels, such as *Amalgamemnon*'s restriction to non-declarative tenses or avoidance of the verb 'to have' in *Next*. In *Subscript* the stylistic/syntactic requirements arose from its representation of the development of forms of consciousness, tracked through pre-biotic then cellular then proto-historic chronology. She worked deliberatively on an infrastructure for this mimesis and produced a paradigm for it, not unlike the expository matrix that Stuart Gilbert laid out in his study of Joyce's *Ulysses*. Eventually she took the view that although the demands on the 'common reader'—indeed, on the ideal reader and her editor—are very heavy she would not publish the schema as part of the novel. She told me on the phone that to have to do this would be like a vote of no confidence in the novel itself. Certainly *Subscript* is an astonishing work of the imagination *per se*, even though she appends a bibliography of the research that lay behind it; but I thought it worth including here a section of the schema ['mya' means million years ago; 'myl' a million years later], in the abbreviated form she wrote up.

Ch.	Title	Time	Period	Creature	Constraints
4	65myl	305-290 mya	Carboniferous	Tetrap. reptile	1st *it* for code or body only. *They/them* for code-sequences, or 'others' [few] + **group.** No

					reflexes [ever]
5	25myl	26-5240mya	Permian	synapsid tds therapsids mammal-like reptiles	*it* for more things / *they* + **Pack**
9	13myl	7mya	Miocene	Chimps: australo-	All pros except I/ me/ my/ he/ him/ His, she/her/hers, reflexives

On first struggling with *Subscript,* on first looking into Chapman's Homer, I told her that she had up-graded historical materialism: Marx grounded his history on species-being but didn't show how species-being evolved in the first place. She had re-instated 'grand narrative'—what grander than this? And that the character Aka—the outsider, stereotype-breaker, culture-critic *avant la lettre* and code-breaker—is surely punning on 'also known as', that is CB-R. At this proposal [only half-teasing this time] Christine/Aka kept an uncharacteristic silence, though she was more responsive to Lorna Sage; see chapter 9 of *Invisible Author.* [I should add that I'm not the blurb-writer referred to on page 62 of those essays; but no names, no pack-drill.] *Subscript* is not only more inventive than Golding's *The Inheritors,* which she thought 'splendid', but has another virtue: it avoids configuring history as lapsarian theology. Christine was familiar enough with Christianity—see *Remake*—but remained a secular humanist.

Barbara and Tim, as it were

Two years before the appearance of *Life, End of,* Jennifer and I were on holiday in Avignon and summoned to visit Christine in Cabrières, a visit that turned out to be the stuff of fiction: we were stuffed into her fiction.

At this stage in her life she had little mobility, few visitors and—as she saw it—few friends. Not surprisingly perhaps, the work she was writing is a tense meditation on the author as character, the one collapsing into and fending off the other. In a letter after our visit, while she was still working on the later chapters, she wondered whether "the paranoiac self aspect isn't clearly enough underlined, since that is what I'm studying." Another friend—"an expert on ambiguity"—had seen the early chapters but "doesn't see that I can't choose one side or the other at this stage, since I'm writing in the present tense [praised by her] and it would simply be bad writing not to leave the ambiguity."

Unaware at the time, Jennifer and I walked straight into this knife-edge work-in-progress. We had, it became clear, gone wrong even before we arrived at Lou Jas: we hadn't followed to the letter her precise instructions about how to get there from Avignon. That taxi-driver had, after all, worked for the local mafia—wasn't it obvious? Then we turned up late at the gate, fumbled the electronic entry procedures and, once in the courtyard, went up the wrong flight of stairs. We were merely a bit embarrassed, while Christine—monitoring each stage of our failures—was hugely irritated: why do people always think they know better, especially if they happen to be a few years younger?

Over tea and cakes the old warmth soon returned and the evening was spent covering the years since we'd last met. Then came the demand: during the night please read the first five chapters of my new book, and give me your one-time editor's report. Little sleep that night, and the next morning Jennifer took off into the village, ostensibly to buy food, while my uneasy 'report' was received. Christine's account of all this—an elaboration, exfoliation, some extenuation—appears in Chapter Six where I ['Tim'] figure as some evasive recidivist in Ingarden's Reader Response Theory. The experience was unnervingly close to that in Malamud's *The Tenants* where Lesser is panicked into a reader's report of his insistent neighbour's manuscript. Jennifer's return from the village was a godsend.

It was a few weeks later we learned we had become the next chapter, the next of her visitor-friends to become textualised. At least Christine sent a draft of the chapter before it went to press, though not of course asking for comment, and I had long retired as editor. Her letter included "The theme as you know goes through several stages, yours, also with two 'annihilations', the first exaggerating the second, but in your case all ends well and you were very generous." Jennifer, as Barbara, emerged unscathed, indeed "a belle-amie". Christine as author was ever one for the dialectic, for the *sic et non*; "Misunderstood both ends. Like the original banal misunderstanding with Tim, quickly repaired" [p.63] and his "somewhat irrelevantly" quoting Yeats is soon turned into a trope "Tim does pinpoint the painpoint. The dancer, the dance, neither of which can dance. The particles of consciousness, however, dance." [p.70] And Empson again, adjusting his villanelle: "It is the brain, it is the brain endures" but assailed by the pain, "the pillars of fire" [p.12], the burning pains in her legs.

If *Remake* was a narratologist's rumination on the narrator's past, chewing the cud on how it seemed and how it might be rendered, then *Life, End of* is more of a meditation by an unwilling reclusive, not calmly meditating but urgently, with each visitor to Lou Jas welcomed and assimilated into her Chapel Perilous, and no holy grails are on offer, least of all for the resident. In the same letter there's a key remark: "The joke here *[in a central set-debate]* is that it's the character lecturing the author, who later reveals that he/she lent his/her knowledge of narratology to the character, as authors do, and so pretended ignorance. These little jokes are what's left of my failed efforts to explain what my life has been devoted to. Don't worry if you don't hear, I'll try and ring thou, it's less tiring than emailing. Love, Christine."

Verse Letter, February 2006

An old age harder than you'd gambled on,
You've lodged yourself the exile that you chose
As concierge and châtelaine of Lou Jas'
Where such, between and through resist repose.

Near blind now offered guidance
On how to read again, you'd peeled
The rhetorics of what we'd read, new
Scalpels cutting open what's congealed.

Your high-walled home fends off most neighbours,
But friends you bricked in, risking rifts
In a final novel's chapter-house whose dean
Gives walk-on parts as tutelary gifts.

Your Bletchley war was put to work again
Tracking the day's transmissions to unmask
Our call-signs, sit-reps, still decoding,
Taking our otherness to task.

Your novels navigate their own street-maps
Not waiting till the walking man goes green,
Powering new lights to play in Plato's cave,
The invisible author shadowed on her screen.

In the park of post-war codes you raised new
Building Regs, Procrustean texts
For Protean tales, but Mira now admits
No subscripts, remakes, brooks no rosy nexts.

[An earlier version was published in *PN Review* volume 33 number 1]

Multitudinous Megafictions:
An Interview with Steven Moore

NICOLAS TREDELL

NICOLAS TREDELL: *Could you start by telling us something about your family background and pre-college schooling?*

STEVEN MOORE: I grew up in southern California, the eldest son in a middle-class family. Neither of my parents went to college, but both were readers, which set a good example. Looking back, I can see two things that set me on the road to becoming a literary critic. When I was seven or eight, my father bought a set of Funk & Wagnalls encyclopedias. I began dipping into it, less for the articles themselves than for the wondrous idea of wrangling the chaos of the world into an orderly set of alphabetical entries. My parents then bought an illustrated set of encyclopedias for children, and that set me to thinking that I'd like to write my own encyclopedia. I decided to focus on famous people, and began typing up my own work, in two justified columns in imitation of the children's version, and freely borrowing from reference books at home and school. I abandoned it after about two years (around age 10), but during that period I not only learned to type, but also unwittingly learned how to write expository prose. Some have praised my critical writing for its clarity, and I owe it all to those early years of childish plagiary.

My father was a research assistant for an oil company, but he made amateur movies on the side: ghost stories, Westerns, short subjects. He did everything—wrote the scripts, shot and edited the films, created the soundtracks—and watching him and occasionally assisting him (even acting in a few of them), I witnessed how art is made, even at that do-it-yourself level, which likewise stood me in good stead when it came time to analyzing how literary works are made.

I read a lot as a kid, but mostly history and biographies, not fiction. Throughout high school I planned to become a history teacher someday, though at that time I was much more into music.

You had a strong interest in rock music and played in bands and composed pieces for performance. How did this develop and how did it relate to your interest in literature?

I was fortunate enough to be a teenager during the glorious Sixties. Like millions of other teens, I fell in love with the rock music of the time, and taught myself to play guitar well enough to join a band. But in another harbinger of my later literary career, I quickly became intrigued by the use of figurative language in some of the more intelligent songs of the time. I still remember listening in the summer of 1966 to Bob Dylan's "I Want You" with puzzled pleasure: the words didn't make *literal* sense, but they made some sort of poetic sense that fascinated me. That's where my literary education began: I was mesmerized by the unexpected things words did in the lyrics of Dylan, Jim Morrison, the Incredible String Band, Procol Harum, even the nonsensical stuff of Syd Barrett and other psychedelic bards. And they led to "legitimate" poets and writers: a reviewer compared the lyrics of the Incredible String Band to Swinburne, so I looked him up in an anthology my father owned and became of fan of his; the Soft Machine—whose lyricist Robert Wyatt remains a favorite to this day—led me to the William Burroughs novel of that title; the group H.P. Lovecraft led me to that eldritch writer, and so on. This growing love of the creative use of language was abetted by some of the poetry I read in high-school English class, where I identified with lines like "I fall upon the thorns of life! I bleed!" (I still remember the line, but I had to Google it just now to learn that it's from Shelley's "Ode to the West Wind.")

In your first two years at college, you were a history major. How did the switch to literature come about?

When I entered college in 1969, I still planned to become a history teacher, but after two years I wasn't so sure. I took a six-month break, and when I resumed at a different university, I decided to switch to English to nurture my growing interest in poetry. I had taken and enjoyed a few creative writing classes during those first two years, which made my decision even easier. But that early interest in history influenced the kind of critic I would become, for I've always been more of a literary historian than a theorist or academic.

While you were a student, you wrote poems for college literary magazines. What kind of poems were these? Were you conscious—or are you conscious in retrospect —of any influences on the poetry you produced then, for example Metaphysical, Romantic, Modernist, Southern Agrarian?

They belonged to the school of undergraduate poesy. I haven't looked at them in 40 years, and don't plan to now, but they were imitative of some of the rock poetry I admired, and in fact many of them were lyrics for my music compositions. I remember writing a few sonnets, and I believe most used rhyme, but they are all best forgotten.

What did you read when you switched majors to English?

At first I took poetry classes, for I didn't have much interest in studying prose. But I experienced an epiphany in the summer of 1972. Allow me to quote from an autobiographical digression in one of my books: "I took only poetry classes until the summer session, when none were on offer and I had to settle for a course called "Techniques of the Novel". Before then I had regarded novels merely as long stories, lacking the "craft or sullen art" of poetry (Dylan Thomas). I can't remember the first novel we read—either *Pamela* or *Joseph Andrews*—but I was impressed when my professor diagrammed the architectural structure of *Tom Jones* on the blackboard. What, novels have structure, like a sonnet? Next up was *Tristram Shandy*, and that did it. It blew my mind, as we said in those days, and by the time I finished the rest of the required reading—*The Old Wives' Tale*, *A Portrait of the Artist as a Young Man*, *To the Lighthouse*, *The Sound and the Fury*—I decided to bid farewell to Dame Poetry and embrace Lord Novel. I got a B in the course.

I also took classes in Middle English and Old English, and enjoyed them enough that I briefly contemplated becoming a medievalist, but one of my teachers told me I'd have to learn Arabic too, so that dissuaded me. By then I was enjoying modern fiction too much anyway. In addition to assigned texts, I was reading contemporary novels on the side, things like *On the Road*, *Catch-22*, *The Crying of Lot 49*, lots of Vonnegut and Brautigan. I was also reading more challenging novelists like Proust and Joyce, and in fact by the time I graduated with an M.A. in 1974, I was a full-out Joyce fanatic. The first critical book I ever purchased was Stuart Gilbert's old book on *Ulysses*, and that started me thinking that I'd like to write something like that someday.

After leaving university and while working as a substitute teacher, you wrote a novel yourself, which is unpublished, and produced a second one of several hundred pages which you abandoned. It may be that, as with your early poetry, you don't particularly want to revisit your fiction, but given the centrality of the novel to your critical and scholarly work, I thought it would be interesting if you could give us an idea of what sort of fiction you were writing at that time.

I was still under Joyce's spell, so the first one, entitled *Clarinets and Candles* (1974–75), was mostly a formal exercise, in which a rather tepid autobiographical tale of unrequited love was enclosed in an elaborate superstructure. I was fascinated by the so-called Linati schema that Gilbert published in his book on *Ulysses*, which shows not only that every chapter has a counterpart in the *Odyssey* but also its own style, color, science/art, etc. So I used sonnet form to construct my novel: not only did it have fourteen chapters, but each chapter ended with a sonnet about clouds (I called them skyscapes), which metaphorically commented on the subject of the preceding chapter. Like *Ulysses* (in the most superficial sense) it boasted lots of literary allusions and stylistic devices; one chapter is in dramatic form, like the Circe episode, and the novel concludes with an epilogue in the form of a fairy tale. All of my time went into the structure and style, neglecting the actual story material, so it deservedly was turned down by the half-dozen publishers I sent it to.

It's a short novel, so I planned to follow it with a *Ulysses*-size novel, also alliteratively titled (*Sunlight and Summer*, 1975–78), which was intended to be a Rabelaisian satire on religion—a subject I was immersed in at the time (and its shadow, the occult). By then I was also under the spell of American meganovels by such authors as Barth, Coover, Gaddis, and Pynchon. It too had a complex structure and showy erudition, but a more sensational plot: it concerned two teenage girls who, after an emotional crisis, become nuns; realizing their mistake after a while, they swing to the other extreme and become prostitutes (while in the background I made lots of snarky remarks about sublimated sexuality in religion), and eventually they abandon the extremes for a more centered approach to life. One of the girls is into vampires, and my research into that subject eventually resulted in an anthology of vampire poetry I edited in the 1980s.

Why did you not persist with writing novels?

I realized I could never be as good as my spellbinding models, plus I was writing literary criticism by that time (I published my first article in 1976), and I realized what talents I had were more suited for the latter. But attempting to write fiction enhanced my appreciation for those who can pull it off, which informed my later criticism and book reviewing. Every book reviewer should try writing a novel before criticizing others.

You weren't able to find a full-time teaching position between 1974 and 1977, or, later, after completing your PhD in 1988. Do you feel this was an advantage or disadvantage in terms of your work as a literary critic and scholar?

It turned out to be an advantage. Had I been hired to teach high school in the 1970s, I probably would have been too busy (and too tired) to write criticism; it's partly because I had some free time on my hands that I began writing. Nor has my lack of a university affiliation prevented me from publishing books with university presses and articles in scholarly journals. (I once attended a conference in France that requested an academic affiliation for the name-badges, so I used Lovecraft's nefarious Miskatonic University—go Ghouls!) I belong to that gypsy tribe known as "independent scholars," and if anything, that status allowed me to write more than I would have otherwise, and more freely, for I've written whatever/whenever I wanted—and never for academic promotion. I also use politically incorrect language—blatantly so in *The Novel: An Alternative History*—which would get me tarred and feathered on many campuses. When writing that work, I sometimes thought it would be nice to be a professor so that I could consult with colleagues in fields outside my own, but looking back, I realize it's probably for the best that no one hired me to teach.

In 1977, you started to work as a bookseller at ABC Books in Denver, and two years later you opened your own bookstore, Moore Books. I know you later worked for Borders, and we can discuss that in due course, but I'd like to focus here on your pre-Borders bookselling experience. What was working as a bookseller and then running your own bookstore like at that time, in the pre-Amazon era? Did it affect the kind of interest you had in literature?

That was a glorious time when anyone could set up a small bookstore without the crushing competition of the big chains or Amazon. It was all very hands-on and un-automated: I called in my orders on a phone, and had little more to go by regarding new books than *Publishers Weekly* and *Books in Print*. It didn't affect my literary tastes, which were pretty much set by that time, but working in a bookstore certainly expands one's general knowledge. You have to be prepared for customers asking for all sorts of things, and "What's the best book on hypnosis?" is not a question every literary scholar can answer. (Nowadays I would recommend *Trance-Migrations* by Lee Siegel.) So I learned a lot about a lot of things, including the economics of book publishing. This experience (and my later career as a publisher) gave me a good sense of how books actually function in the real world, the influence of reviews, the wide range of reader expectations, etc., all of which has kept me grounded over the years. Some critics write about literature in such abstruse, theoretical terms that I suspect they've lost sight of how and why authors write books, and why and how people read them.

Moore Books was a small shop (with a black cat named Montague), and business was modest enough that I wrote my first book during that period. By that time I realized that the store would never generate enough income to live comfortably, so I decided to return to university and earn a PhD and try again to become a teacher. As it happens, I sold my store at the right time, for two years later a huge Barnes & Noble opened a half mile away, which would have wiped me out.

While you were working as a bookseller and studying for a PhD, you were developing your career as a literary critic. You wrote and published scholarly essays and reviews and your first book, A Reader's Guide to William Gaddis's The Recognitions, *came out in 1982. You followed this up by co-editing and contributing to an essay collection,* In Recognition of William Gaddis, *which appeared in 1984, edited an anthology called* Vampire in Verse, *which was exposed to the light of day in 1985, and wrote an authoritative monograph on Gaddis which Twayne brought out in its United States Authors series in 1989 and which Bloomsbury reissued, in an expanded edition, in early 2015. Could you talk about the progress of your career as a critic during the 1980s, especially the growth of your interest in Gaddis?*

I first learned of William Gaddis in the fall of 1975. I read a review in my father's *Time* magazine of Gaddis's newly published *J R*, which had a sidebar on a new edition of his 1955 novel *The Recognitions*. That caught my eye because the reviewer compared it to *Ulysses*, which was all I needed to hear, for I was in the depths of my Joyce addiction. I found a copy locally and bought it the next day, read it shortly after, and was blown away by it. As I wrote in the preface to my *Reader's Guide*:

> As is my custom when confronted with exhilarating literature, I began looking around to see what kind of critical work had been done on the novel, fully expecting to find mountains of material (and silently wondering all the time how I had missed hearing of such a novel). To my utter dismay, I found not mountains but molehills, and this in 1975, a full twenty years after publication. Apparently the novel had been sitting like an island in the stream of American literature, circumnavigated a few times, but as yet unexplored. Feeling let down by the academic scholarly community, I proceeded to write (for myself if no one else) the kind of book someone should have written long ago.

> It also struck me that writing the first book on Gaddis would be better than writing the 101st book on Joyce, which I was contemplating. I was so taken by Gaddis that I wrote quite a bit about him in the 1980s and began collecting his letters for the edition I eventually published in 2013. I continue to regard him as one of the greatest American novelists of the second half of the twentieth century. And that notion of writing about an author who has been undeservedly neglected stuck with me, for in later years I sort of specialized in such authors (Chandler Brossard, Alexander Theroux, David Markson, W. M. Spackman, and others).

> The 1980s were an incredibly busy time for me. In addition to earning a PhD between 1983 and 1988, I wrote or edited

the four books you mention, plus a dozen or so essays and introductions to books, along with dozens of book reviews. After I joined Dalkey Archive Press in 1988, I began slowing down because I didn't have time for much beyond book reviews.

Could I pick up a general point in your 1989 book on Gaddis? You say in Chapter 5: "What is lacking in more compact critiques of American manners and mores—Fitzgerald's The Great Gatsby, *say, or Pynchon's* The Crying of Lot 49—*is the breadth and density of detail that give J R its greater weight and plausibility, comprehensiveness & exactitude. Gaddis's novel is as witty as Fitzgerald's and as fantastic as Pynchon's, but easily outdistances either as a critique of the American dream due to the 'detail & development' that Gaddis, like Flaubert, pursues with such encyclopedic thoroughness" (p. 97). But I wonder here about your elevation of the encyclopedic over the compact novel—or, to use other terms, the novel of saturation over the novel of selection? It could be argued that the two kinds of novel are both effective but in different ways. Gatsby, for example, has generated an enormous amount of commentary and interpretation that suggests it is a comprehensive critique of the American Dream and of much else, but in a compressed form that the reader has to work to draw out.*

I totally agree that both modes—the novel of encyclopedic saturation vs. compact selection—are equally valid and effective, and in fact the shorter novels deliver more of an emotional punch because they are condensed. That's certainly the case with *The Great Gatsby*, which I reread recently and admired more than ever. It's just a personal choice: though some of my favorite novelists (Firbank, Spackman) wrote very short novels, I've always preferred huge flamboyant novels over short ones.

In Chapter 7 of the Gaddis book, you identify in his novels not only the "theme of personal failure" but "the larger theme of the failure of America itself [...] Throughout his work [...] there is a feeling of bitter disappointment at America's failure to fulfill its potential, to live up to the magnificent expectations held for the New World ever since Columbus declared it the Terrestrial Paradise predicted by Scripture" (p. 136). Do you yourself endorse the idea that America has failed "to fulfill its potential" and do you share this "feeling of disappointment"?

I do indeed. One mundane reason I like Gaddis's novels is that I share many of his views, and like many Americans today, I'm rather ashamed at the way my country has turned out. This is especially the case with my generation: in the 1960s there were hopes and expectations that the country would make a great leap forward, especially with the advances in civil rights and other liberation movements (women's, gay, Native Americans). The dawning of the Age of Aquarius, and all that. But the bulk of the country turned its back on those ideals, and the country has been going downhill ever since. Though I'll admit I'd rather live here than many places, if only because I can get away with anti-patriotic sentiments like these (and the anti-religious statements that follow) without fear of being arrested.

You said earlier that Sunlight and Summer, *the second novel you started, was intended as a Rabelaisian satire on religion and that you were immersed in religion—and its shadow, the occult—at that time. I wondered if we might explore your attitude to religion further, taking up an observation you make in Chapter 6 of the Gaddis book, where you say: "The crucial difference is that literary and legal fictions are recognized as fictions; religious fictions are not. Fundamentalists, [McCandless] implies, are like poor readers who first mistake a work of fiction for fact, then impose their literal-minded misreadings on others— at gunpoint, if necessary" (p. 132). Of course, you're explicating Carpenter's* Gothic *here but I'd like to ask if you yourself thought that the problem with religious beliefs, particularly of a fundamentalist kind, is that they are not recognized as fictions.*

Exactly, which is to say the so-called sacred scriptures those beliefs are based on are fictions (not just the Bible, of course, but the Quran, the Book of Mormon, the Vedas, the narrative Buddhist sutras, etc.). As in novels, there are some admirable ethical lessons to be learned from them, but to mistake them as the pronouncements of a god rather than what they are—the writings of men, many of whom we would now call religious fanatics—leads to all sorts of problems, as the headlines of any newspaper will show. I've been an atheist since I was a teenager, but I've been fascinated all my life with how religions came about. Most of my reading was on the history of religion—textual histories of sacred books, comparative religion, its relation with supernaturalism and the occult, mythology, etc.—not theology per se, which I regard as worthless because its fundamental premise (the existence of a god) is an error, which invalidates everything that follows, just as if you were to begin a long, complex equation with "Since $2 + 3 = 6$, then . . ." For me it's as simple as that, but most believers equate religion with communal solidarity, morality, ethnocentrism, psychological needs, comfort-food solace, and so on, which complicates things.

You mentioned earlier that you joined Dalkey Archive Press in 1988 and that this left you little time for writing criticism. You worked at Dalkey from 1988 to 1996 and in that period you were also managing editor of The Review of Contemporary Fiction, *which Dalkey published. Could you tell us about Dalkey Archive Press and your experience of working there?*

The Review of Contemporary Fiction was founded by John O'Brien in 1981, and I began contributing to it the following year. He started Dalkey Archive in 1984 as a means of reprinting some of his favorite novels, and by 1987 it had grown large enough that he felt he needed another person to help, and he invited me to join. Since I was striking out in my job search for a teaching position and was broke, I accepted his invitation. I had never planned to become a publisher, but I liked some of the books Dalkey had already published, and figured this would be a good way for me too to reprint some of my own favorite authors. The work was very time-consuming at first, because I had to do a little of everything: copyedit books, design the covers, see them through the press, work with sales reps and book review editors to get them noticed, write catalog copy, attend trade shows, create ads, explore fundraising possibilities—plus edit/publish three issues of the *Review* a year. Like all small presses, we had trouble getting the media to review our books and stores to stock them, so it was always an uphill battle. O'Brien was difficult to work with —the archetypal boss from hell—and that, along with the deep depression I had fallen into in 1985, combined to make my Dalkey years a rather miserable period, despite the rewards of getting some deserving authors into print. Another plus was that I could review whatever I wanted in the *Review*; Michael Dirda of the *Washington Post* saw and liked my reviews and invited me to start writing for it, which I've been doing two or three times a year ever since 1990.

Your Wikipedia entry attributes your resignation from Dalkey to "irreconcilable differences with the publisher". Is this accurate and, if so, would you like to say any more about those differences?

That is indeed accurate, and suffice it to say that when I left in 1996, two-thirds of the staff left for the same reason: no one could stand working for O'Brien. I was getting a little tired of the publishing business anyway, but I would have stuck it out had he not been such a %@#&@$!

You were an early enthusiast for the work of David Foster Wallace. How did your interest in his fiction start and develop?

I read his first novel, *The Broom of the System*, when it came out in 1987 and I knew right away he was a major talent and destined for greatness. As it happened, O'Brien had just asked me to guest-edit a special issue of the *Review* called "The Novelist as Critic", so I invited Wallace to contribute an essay, which he did. We started corresponding, and then I asked him to contribute to another issue on David Markson. (Both were reprinted in his posthumous collection *Both Flesh and Not*.) After Dalkey Archive moved at the invitation of Charles Harris of Illinois State University from the suburbs of Chicago to Normal, Illinois, in the summer of 1992, Charlie told me there was an opening for a creative writing teacher there, in case I knew of anyone. I informed Dave, he applied, and was accepted for the position in 1993. That December he asked me to read the draft of *Infinite Jest* to suggest cuts, an experience I've written about at length elsewhere. Regrettably, we didn't see much of each other during the years we lived in the same town—because of my depression I didn't feel like socializing—though he occasionally dropped by the Dalkey office to talk, and once we played tennis. We kept in touch after I left Dalkey in 1996—he sent me the stories that later made up *Brief Interviews with Hideous Men* in batches as he wrote them, hoping I'd like them (which I certainly did)—and we exchanged the occasional letter or postcard until around 2004. Needless to say, his suicide in 2008 hit me hard.

In 1996, after resigning from Dalkey, you went back to bookselling, working for Borders Books and Music. What was this like, particularly in relation to your previous experience of bookselling?

It was completely different. The first bookstore I worked for was a family-run business with about five employees, and my own store was a one-man operation where I had to do everything. In some ways it was nice to be a cog in a big machine, where I didn't have to worry about daily receipts or whether I could pay my bills on time. There were some corporate policies I didn't care for, but the atmosphere was much more cheerful than Dalkey —by that time I had crawled out of my long depression—and I enjoyed the generous employee discount and benefits. From almost the beginning, however, I had my eye on a job at the corporate office, and in 2001 I applied for a book buyer's position and was hired. After leaving Dalkey in 1996 I had moved back to my hometown in Colorado, so I packed up again and moved to Ann Arbor, Michigan, into the same apartment I'm typing these words in. I worked there until January of 2010, when I was caught up in one of the waves of layoffs before Borders finally went under in 2011.

And you resumed writing criticism during those early years with Borders?

Yes. I began writing a few essays when working at the bookstore in Colorado, and in 2001 I published *Beerspit Night and Cursing: The Correspondence of Charles Bukowksi and Sheri Martinelli.* (She was an old girlfriend of Gaddis's and an intriguing character in her own right. I've never cared for Bukowksi: I did the book just to get Martinelli's letters into print.) In 2004, bored and needing something to do during my free time, I decided to write a history of the novel; I figured that should keep me busy for a while. Working at the home office of Borders was a godsend; as a buyer, I could request all the books I needed for my work from publishers' sales reps, who were happy to oblige (or so they said), thus saving thousands of dollars over the years, especially with pricey university press publications. Also, the University of Michigan in Ann Arbor boasts a stupendous research library. I almost literally could not have written my history anywhere else and/or at any other time in my life, so once again, things worked out for the best. It's almost enough to make an atheist like me believe in providence.

Could we explore that momentous decision to write a history of the novel? I know that in your introduction to volume one of The Novel: An Alternative History *(2010), you recall that you "began thinking seriously of writing it" in 2002 when you discovered Francesco Colonna's* Hypnerotomachia Poliphili *[Poliphi's Erotic Dream-Quest, 1499] and read B. R. Myers, Dale Peck and Jonathan Franzen's "three-pronged attack on the kind of fiction I love" (p. 1). In the context of this interview and from your current vantage point, could you revisit the process that led you to start writing your alternative history of the novel in earnest?*

As I explain in that introduction, I first started thinking about the topic in the early 1990s when working at Dalkey Archive, for our books didn't fit in with the so-called great tradition of the novel—the realistic works that continue to be thought of as the norm—but rather followed an older tradition that went back from Joyce to Sterne to Rabelais and Boccaccio (with numerous sidetrips), all the way back to Petronius' *Satyricon*. I realized that avant-garde, experimental fiction was not a twentieth-century aberration (as some would have it) but an alternative approach that has always existed. At any given time in history, the majority of writers (and artists, composers, movie-makers, et al.) follow the conventions of their era, while a minority explores new options, and it's that group that has always interested me. In the later 1990s I jotted down some notes on what a book on the subject might entail, and continued to think about it (as you note) during the new millennium. I kept dragging my feet about actually starting, but what finally lit a fire under me was Roddy Doyle's attack on Joyce in a newspaper article in early 2004, for he denigrated not only Joyce but (by implication) all experimental novelists like him—all my pretty ones. That's when I decided to get down to work.

The two volumes of The Novel: An Alternative History *are an immense feat of reading, research, analysis, synthesis and writing, running to around 1700 pages in all and covering a vast amount of literary, cultural, historical and geographical ground. You've mentioned how valuable it was to be able to get books through your position at Borders and to have access to the University of Michigan library in Ann Arbor, but it would be interesting if you could tell us more about how you approached this epic task.*

Instead of spending a year or so researching and outlining the book, as a normal person would, I just dove right in, illustrating Pope's observation that "fools rush in where angels fear to tread". I dashed off the truculent introduction in about a week, airing grievances against conservative, narrow-minded critics that had been building up ever since 1975 when I discovered how critics had trashed Gaddis's *Recognitions*. I was aware that literary fiction began with the ancient Egyptians and Assyrians, and also knew that portions of the Bible had been compared to novels, so I began there and just sort of educated myself as I went along. For each section, I sought out some scholarly overviews of the period, worked up a reading list of what to cover, then started reading and writing, glancing from time to time at further scholarship to keep me on track. As I progressed and learned more, I sometimes backtracked and revised accordingly, and by the time I finished each section I was confident that I had attained a good working knowledge of a period. I was delighted when a historian of Chinese literature wrote me after the first volume appeared and said that my survey of early Chinese novels was the best non-specialist account he'd ever read. That's all my book was intended to be: not a definitive history but a reasonably informed overview, with special attention to the technical advances in fiction-writing that link premodern novelists with postmodern ones.

You say in your Introduction to the first volume that "the challenge for me is not unfamiliarity with earlier literature but with foreign languages" and that "I've had to rely on translations for all but a handful of the novels discussed in this book—a major drawback for someone like me in it for the language" (p. 36). But you still felt it was worth persisting with the project despite this "major drawback"?

Yes. See "fools rush in" remark above. No critic knows enough languages to write a global history like this, which is probably why no one had previously attempted one, but I thought I'd give it a try. It helped that the last 40 years have seen a profusion of good translations of world literature, though I complain in my pages of many omissions and inadequacies.

The Novel: An Alternative History is large and contains multitudes but this also provokes what seems to be the most central objection to it—that it is too capacious, a kind of loose, baggy monster with definitions that tend to slide around. For example, in the first paragraph of your section on "Medieval Icelandic Fiction", you assert that, when they started writing the sagas, "Icelandic writers basically invented the social realist novel, some 600 years before Balzac introduced the genre in continental Europe" (p. 147). But in the last paragraph of the same section you contend "The sagas may not resemble mainstream novels but they do resemble modernist ones, that is, the novels that dispensed with the cosy moralizing and sociological padding of Victorian novels" (164). So Icelandic sagas are both Balzacian and modernist, social realist and non-mainstream. I know there are ways in which these apparent contradictions might be reconciled, but aren't they indicative of the way in which your approach licenses a certain looseness that risks effacing the specific qualities of particular literary works?

I see what you mean, but after pointing out how elastic the term "novel" is, how unsatisfactory all definitions of the novel are, how resistant to consensus the novel genre is even regarding basic features like page length, prose vs. poetry, fictional vs. nonfictional content, etc.—because of all this, I didn't feel that I needed to be rigidly precise in my terminology. The novel genre is capacious and amorphous, so I felt justified in taking a freewheeling, Whitmanesque approach (to pick up on your allusion), at the risk of some terminological imprecision. (What was that Walt said about contradicting himself?) Because in fact Icelandic novels display *both* Balzacian and modernist features, realistic and supernatural elements, as well as some specific to Icelandic fiction. And in my defence, I spend more time discussing "the specific qualities of particular literary works" than in making sweeping generalizations like the ones you quote. It's the opposite of the approach Michael McKeon takes in *The Origins of the English Novel*, where he begins by writing brilliantly about English literary culture in the seventeenth century but discusses only a handful of English novels, whereas I discuss about 50 published during that century.

I might add that before I began writing it, I thought it would be wonderful someday to write a huge, outlandish book along the lines of Burton's *Anatomy of Melancholy*, Frazer's *Golden Bough*, and Graves's *White Goddess*—"loose, baggy monsters" filled with forgotten lore and heterodox opinions that are appealing despite their eccentricity, if not *because* of their eccentricity. I wouldn't put my two-volume study in their league, but those are the kinds of books—as opposed to standard literary criticism —that were my models.

Could I take up a point Alberto Manguel makes in a largely favourable review of the first volume of The Novel: An Alternative History *in the* Washington Post *(22 Aug 2010), where he says: "As astute and thorough as this book is, however, it is based on a tenuous premise: That 'the standard history of the novel' states that the form 'was born in 18th-century England'. This is not quite fair: A whole library of histories of the novel has traced the genre's origins to the same ancient sources that Moore discusses. Margaret Anne Doody's* The True History of the Novel *(1996) is perhaps the best known, but in the 1930s, Dorothy L. Sayers was tracking the detective novel back to the Bible and the Greeks. In the 1890s, Spanish scholars searched for models of Don Quixote in ancient tales such as the* Alexander Romance *and the Kalilah and Dimnah story cycle". How would you respond to Manguel's point?*

Manguel grossly exaggerates the familiarity of general readers with the premodern novel, and that's who the book was written for, not for specialists in the field. *The Novel* was written, priced, and marketed as a *trade* book, not as an academic monograph. Manguel is an uncommonly well-read man, as anyone who has explored his delightfully erudite *Dictionary of Imaginary Places* knows; more common is the response of British novelist Nicola Barker, whom my publisher approached for a blurb: puzzled by the first volume's subtitle ("Beginnings to 1600"), she said she always thought Samuel Richardson invented the novel with *Pamela*. I cite Moody and other historians of the novel throughout my book; my job was to synthesize all the findings of specialists, mostly buried in obscure journals and academic monographs, and popularize this material for a general educated audience. But even specialists are unfamiliar with much of this material: I'm sure those Spanish scholars who stumbled upon the *Alexander Romance* had no idea what was going on in early Chinese fiction during Cervantes' time, and even today I doubt specialists in the early Sanskrit novel, say, are familiar with Byzantine novels of the twelfth century, or Icelandic scholars with medieval Tibetan fiction. I mean, how familiar were *you* with all this material before you picked up my book?

There's another criticism of The Novel: An Alternative History *that relates to a topic we discussed earlier in this interview—your attitude to religion. In the* Boston Review *(17 March 2014), for example, Roger Boylan, again in a largely favourable review, says "Moore's lucid criticism is frequently derailed by his dislike of religion" and that this dislike "threatens to upset his composure; he seems constitutionally incapable of finding any redeeming value in the 2,000-year history of Christianity that has been so much a part of Western culture". Steven Donoghue, in the online journal* Open Letters Monthly, *similarly finds your aversion to religion, which he compares to that of Richard Dawkins and Christopher Hitchens, "as ubiquitous as it is discordant in a long work of literary history". What would you say to that kind of criticism?*

I began writing the book in 2004, only a few years after some deeply religious people crashed two planes into the World Trade Center—a "faith-based initiative", as someone bitterly quipped—and in 2004 religious conservatives played a large role in re-electing the worst president in American history (not uncoincidentally a born-again Christian), in keeping with their ongoing efforts to shut down abortion clinics and to remove Harry Potter books from school libraries for promoting witchcraft. So my dislike of religion was at a boiling point by that time. And by the way I find it hypocritical, if not cowardly, of academics to censure any whiff of sexism, racism, misogyny, homophobia, intolerance, patriarchalism, predatory capitalism, imperialism, or colonialism in the authors they write about, but to remain silent when it comes to religion, which is a major contributor to all of the above.

When I began writing, I didn't plan to be so aggressively anti-religious, but the topic was hard to ignore because religion is a big presence in premodern fiction. I also quickly realized that literature is a kind of secular scripture that co-exists with sacred scripture, sometimes complementing it, sometimes challenging it. Morality in sacred books is black and white: do this, don't do that. But creative writers know that life is fifty or more shades of grey. The Bible says don't steal, but Victor Hugo comes along and asks what if a man steals bread for his starving relations? It struck me that many early novelists were dramatizing the pronouncements in sacred scripture in order to test them out in real-life scenarios, and more often than not exposed their inadequacy in the process. So if you read books partly for guidance on how to live, you are better served by secular rather than sacred literature. Plus fiction only pretends to be real, unlike sacred literature, which insists on its nonfictional status and has a nasty history of burning or beheading anyone who challenges its veracity.

As in a formal debate, or better yet a courtroom, it's not enough to present your case: you need to demolish your opponent's case in order to strengthen yours. So I took every opportunity to ridicule religion, largely for the sake of my thesis, but also because I believe every person should speak out against outrages when the opportunity arises. My lifetime of study of religion taught me that religion is a history of outrages—against reason, to begin with—so I adopted Voltaire's *écrasez l'infâme* as my motto. I'm more than happy to be associated with people like Hitchens and Dawkins: we're on the right side of history.

In your introduction to The Novel: An Alternative History, *you have some animadversions on French literary theorists, whom you hold "largely responsible for turning literary criticism into the laughingstock it's become to most people outside the profession; 40 years ago they sashayed over like flirty foreign-exchange students and began seducing English and American critics into making fools of themselves" (p. 20). But isn't your attitude here similar to the attitude of those who denounce "difficult" fiction because a mass audience supposedly finds it incomprehensible and risible? Couldn't one say that literary theory, like literature, is not for everyone but no less valuable because of that and that some readers enjoy its intricacies as you might enjoy those of experimental fiction? Furthermore, couldn't one argue that there is some convergence between literary theory and the kind of fiction you like? For instance, when you state, in the chapter in your Gaddis book on* Carpenter's Gothic, *"All the world's a text, Gaddis implies, and all the men and women merely readers" (pp. 132-3), this sounds close to a position that one might derive from Jacques Derrida. And one could contend that such theory, for some people, might help to illuminate Gaddis's work, make it more approachable.*

Literature can be as complicated as it wants to be, but I think criticism should be lucid and intelligible, which most theory-driven criticism is not. Some obviously "enjoy its intricacies," but I don't; that's not what I turn to criticism for. Perhaps it's because I consider myself a scholar rather than an academic. Scholarship represents the older approach to literary criticism, which basically means working outward from the text: you start with the words on the page, look up the ones you don't know (and trace allusions, quotations, and sources if need be), note the patterns of imagery and structural devices, and work your way up to an explanation of how it all works together, which should result in an appreciation of the writer's artistry. Since the 1970s academics seem to work from the outside in: they start with a trendy topic, master the specialized lingo and theory associated with it (often shanghaied from a non-literary field), and then find a text on which they can apply that notion—often resulting not in appreciation but in an exposure of the artist's alleged shortcomings. It's like inventing a new tool, and then looking around for something to use it on, rather than the older way of starting with a text and then choosing the appropriate tools to open it up for inspection.

And the language those academics use! So ugly, so tone-deaf, so needlessly obscure. Sixty years ago, any educated person could pick up the latest issue of the *Journal of English and Germanic Philology* and read it as though it were the latest issue of *Time* magazine, but nowadays one has to struggle to get through the jargon-laden, obfuscatory prose of academic critics, rarely emerging with new insights into a work of art. I remember being puzzled when I first saw that stuff in the late 1970s; I'd finish an article in the *James Joyce Quarterly* and say, "Well I guess you *could* look at it that way, though I don't know why anyone would want to." I was always reminded of Horatio's response to one of Hamlet's convoluted notions: "'Twere to consider too curiously to consider so." (Translation: Dude, you're overthinking it!) How appropriate that one of the meanings of "academic" (as in, "it's an academic question") is "having no practical or useful significance" (*Merriam-Webster Collegiate Dictionary*, 11th edn). To be sure, most academics are very smart people, and I've read some ingenious stuff by them, but working in an ivory tower and communicating only with fellow academics can sometimes cause them to lose sight of how and why literature is written. The forgotten British novelist Storm Jameson put it better in *Parthian Words* (1970), where she warned critics against "the dangers of retreating into a Platonic realm of forms and essences where the practice of criticism is neglected for the pleasures of constructing scholastically intricate general theories addressed to the circle of initiates."

I'm sure you've seen the steady stream of books and articles assessing the damage done to literary studies by theory-driven academics, who are even held responsible for declining enrollments in university English programs, and who are routinely ridiculed in the press. The *New York Times* used to cover the annual MLA convention, and would report back on papers alleging masturbation imagery in Jane Austen, etc. with ill-concealed scorn. Forty years ago, literary critics belonged to a club I wanted to join, but the younger me would not want to join today's version of that club.

You've engaged closely with contemporary fiction and you write in an up-to-date idiom but, looking at your critical career, it seems closer in some ways to that of a nineteenth- or early twentieth-century person of letters than to that of a modern academic. In this context, it was intriguing to find that in your introduction to The Novel: An Alternative History *you call the English literary historian, biographer and critic George Saintsbury (1845-1933) "my idol" (p. 35). Why do you idolize Saintsbury and have you tried to emulate him in any way?*

Like the older "scholar" label, I'm happy to be identified with the older man of letters tag, and who better exemplifies that than George Saintsbury? He was unbelievably well-read, yet wore his erudition lightly. Reading him is like sitting in an old-fashioned English club, brandy snifter in hand, listening to a charming literary raconteur. In his analysis of literature, he knew exactly what snippets of biography were relevant, indulged in occasional personal anecdotes and admissions of love for some female characters, and always brilliantly contextualized and judged whatever author he was writing about. Here's a random example, in which he's evaluating Thomas Lovell Beddoes: "He is a younger and tragic counterpart to Charles Lamb in the intensity with which he has imbibed the Elizabethan spirit, rather from the nightshade of Webster and Tourneur than from the vine of Shakespeare" (*A History of Nineteenth Century Literature*). Do you see how much reading and taste goes into a casual comparison like that, not to mention the lilting cadence and evocative use of botanical imagery? And how sublime is his observation on Voltaire's usage of "Mademoiselle" Cunégonde in *Candide*: "nobody will ever know anything about style who does not feel what the continual repetition in Candide's mouth of the 'Mademoiselle' does" (*A History of the French Novel*)? He knew everything about style, both how to evaluate it and how to use it himself. His books were published by commercial houses like Macmillan rather than by university presses, and could be read by anyone with a high-school education. So yes, I attempted to emulate him, but I was more mindful of writers like Hunter S. Thompson, Anthony Lane of the *New Yorker*, rock critics like Lester Bangs, and especially David Foster Wallace's nonfiction. Have you read his book on the history of infinity? If he had decided instead to write a history of the novel, I like to think the result would have resembled mine (minus the atheistic ranting), though I'm as far below his level as I am from Saintsbury's.

Coming back to twentieth-century fiction, do you have any thoughts on the innovative British novelists who emerged in the 1960s, such as Christine Brooke-

Rose, Alan Burns, B. S. Johnson and Ann Quin, all of whom featured at one time or another in The Review of Contemporary Fiction? *They aroused some initial interest but were soon marginalized, and both Johnson and Quin died early, Johnson definitely and Quin possibly by suicide. But there has been growing retrospective interest in the UK, particularly in Brooke-Rose, the inspiration of Verbivoracious Press, and Johnson, the subject of Jonathan Coe's major biography in 2004. How did they—and how do they—impinge on the American alternative fiction scene?*

I read with admiration several Brooke-Rose novels in the 1980s—I think I read all four in that Carcanet omnibus—and I liked *Amalgamemnon* enough to reprint it when I was at Dalkey Archive. While there I also published what I believe is one of the first critical monographs on her work, Friedman and Martin's *Utterly Other Discourse* (1995). I haven't read Burns or Quin—they were featured in the *Review* after I left—but I've read Johnson's novel-in-a-box *The Unfortunates* and I love his use of typography in *House Mother Normal*. I don't know how they impinged on American fiction at that time: I would guess they had minimal influence because most of their books were available only in British editions and not readily available here. Among that generation of British novelists I also read a lot of Brigid Brophy, whose *In Transit* in particular is fabulous. I edited an issue of the *Review* on her, but sadly it appeared two months after she died in August 1995.

The two volumes of The Novel: An Alternative History *make up an immensely rich and substantial work that is, as you indicated earlier, unparalleled in its coverage; but its very strengths leave its enthusiastic readers wanting you to continue this story of so many stories. In your interview with Jeff Bursey dated 26 November 2013, almost two years ago, you say that you "have a clear idea of what a third volume would entail" and that you wouldn't undertake it now because of the huge amount of work that it would involve. You go on to say that you've "lost interest in writing criticism in general". Would those two statements still be true today, in October 2015?*

I'm afraid so. I've written a few short essays since then, and I continue to review new books for the *Washington Post*, but I don't have any desire to take on new writing projects. In the winter of 2013–14 a burst of energy allowed me to update that 1989 book on William Gaddis you've quoted, but that was more a case of tying up loose ends than a recommitment to criticism.

What about other kinds of writing? You write with acumen, verve and wit; you've had an unusually varied and interesting life; you've met a wide range of people, especially authors, including such major novelists as William Gaddis and David Foster Wallace. Any memoir you wrote would surely be fascinating. Would you contemplate doing that?

No. I would welcome an opportunity to collect all my miscellaneous essays and reviews into a big book—especially since they cover many of the authors I planned to treat in the third volume of my novel-history— but as I said I have no desire to write anything new.

Could I ask finally whether, in light of your wide experience in writing, editing, publishing and selling books, and your profound and wide-ranging knowledge of fiction from ancient times to the present, you have any reflections on the current state and future of the novel—especially, given your own interests, the difficult, experimental, innovative novel - in the era of digital culture, of the internet, e-books and Amazon?

Much to my surprise and delight, the kinds of novels I prefer continue to be published, though I suspect the audience for them is shrinking. Just this year (2015) there appeared several "difficult, experimental, innovative novels," such as Reif Larsen's *I Am Radar*, Joshua Cohen's *Book of Numbers*, William T. Vollmann's *The Dying Grass*, and the first two 800-page volumes of Mark Z. Danielewski's *The Familiar*. Translations of big, innovative novels are also appearing regularly: last year saw Leopold Marechal's *Adam Buenosayres*—which inspired one of the few short essays

I've written recently—as well as the first volume of Miklós Szentkuthy's enormous *Prae*, and Dalkey is reportedly publishing soon John Woods's translation of Arno Schmidt's *Bottom's Dream*, for which I've been waiting all my adult life. (Literally: I first learned of it in the mid-1970s in the context of *Finnegans Wake*, whose difficulty it rivals.) And there's no let-up in shorter experimental novels: if anything, more than ever are appearing nowadays thanks to recent print-on-demand technology and do-it-yourself publishing. So experimental novels, big and small, are alive and well, but as I say I suspect the genre is approaching the status of poetry—that is, a literary form that appeals only to a limited, select audience. But as long as such novels continue to appear, I'll be content.

October 2015

Steven Moore Bibliography

NON-FICTION

A Reader's Guide to William Gaddis's "The Recognitions." Lincoln: University of Nebraska Press, 1982.

William Gaddis. Boston: Twayne, 1989. Expanded edition: New York: Bloomsbury, 2015.

Ronald Firbank: An Annotated Bibliography of Secondary Materials, 1905-1995. Normal, IL: Dalkey Archive Press, 1996.

The Novel: An Alternative History, Beginnings to 1600. New York: Continuum, 2010.

The Novel: An Alternative History, 1600-1800. New York and London: Bloomsbury, 2013.

ESSAYS AND ARTICLES

"'Parallel, Not Series': Thomas Pynchon and William Gaddis." *Pynchon Notes* 11 (February 1983): 6–26.

"Alexander Theroux's *Darconville's Cat* and the Tradition of Learned Wit." *Contemporary Literature* 27 (Summer 1986): 233–45.

"Chandler Brossard: An Introduction and Checklist." *Review of Contemporary Fiction* [RCF] 7.1 (Spring 1987): 58–86.

"Introduction." Alan Ansen, *Contact Highs: Selected Poems 1957-1987.* Elmwood Park, IL: Dalkey Archive, 1989. xi-xxxiv.

"David Markson and the Art of Allusion." *RCF* 10.2 (Summer 1990): 164–78.

"Alexander Theroux: An Introduction." *RCF* 11.1 (Spring 1991): 7-28.

"Fin de Siècle." *American Notes & Queries* 5.4 (October 1992): 223–24. Rpt. in *Surfing Tomorrow: Essays on the Future of American Fiction.* Ed. Lance Olsen. Prairie Village, KS: Potpourri, 1995. 69–70.

"Brigid Brophy: An Introduction and Checklist." *RCF* 15.3 (Fall 1995): 7–

11.

"A New Language for Desire: *Aureole*." *RCF* 17.3 (Fall 1997): 206–14.

"Sheri Martinelli: A Modernist Muse." *Gargoyle* 41 (Summer 1998): 29–54.

"Nympholepsy." *Gargoyle* 45 (October 2002): 9–22.

"The First Draft Version of *Infinite Jest*." Howling Fantods website, posted 9 May 2003. http://www. thehowlingfantods.com/ij_first.htm

"Paper Flowers: Richard Brautigan's Poetry." In *Richard Brautigan: Essays on the Writings and Life*. Ed. John F. Barber. Jefferson, NC: McFarland & Co., 2006. 188–204.

"In Memoriam David Foster Wallace." *Modernism/Modernity* 16.1 (January 2009): 1–3.

"Alexander Theroux—*Darconville's Cat*." *The Syllabus*. Ed. G. N. Forester and M. J. Nicholls. Singapore: Verbivoracious Press, 2015. 107–8.

"Maximalism Down Argentine Way: *Adam Buenosayres*." *Pleasure* no. 4 (October 2015): 25–29.

EDITED

With John R. Kuehl. *In Recognition of William Gaddis*. Syracuse: Syracuse University Press, 1984.

The Vampire in Verse. Dracula Press, 1985.

Edward Dahlberg. *Samuel Beckett's Wake and Other Uncollected Prose*. Elmwood Park, IL: Dalkey Archive Press, 1989.

The Early Firbank. London: Quartet, 1991.

W. M. Spackman, *Complete Fiction*. Normal, IL: Dalkey Archive, 1997.

Beerspit Night and Cursing: The Correspondence of Charles Bukowski and Sheri Martinelli. Santa Rosa, CA: Black Sparrow, 2001.

Chandler Brossard, *Over the Rainbow? Hardly: Selected Short Seizures*. Northville, MI: Sun Dog Press, 2005.

The Letters of William Gaddis. Champaign, IL: Dalkey Archive Press, 2013.

Towards an Aesthetic of Obscenity and Grace: Jeff Nuttall's Avant-Garde Fiction

DOUGLAS FIELD

As hangovers go, Jeff Nuttall's was atomic. By the early 1970s, the visceral, oscillating energy of the previous decade—"all things coming under my senses quivered with a crazy potential"—had transformed into lethargy and emptiness.[1] During the 1960s the future had been a void; for H-bomb society members, certainty had been eviscerated. It was, Nuttall recalled, "a perpetual noon of decisions, every action crucial being possibly final," a period of amaranthine now that demanded a rupture with the past as well as the future: "Art lives when values melt," Nuttall declared in the 1960s: "if you want to exist you must accept the flesh and the moment."[2]

By the early 1970s, Nuttall acknowledged that the atomic political-creative energy of the 1960s ended, not with a bang, but a whimper—"a revolution that went off at half-cock"—an experience he documented in *Bomb Culture*, a seminal account of 1960s underground subcultures, a book in which Nuttall attempted to say farewell to that scene, but a work that "had the effect of associating . . . [him] *with* the underground."[3] As he observed in the introduction to his 1975 novel *The House Party*, the early seventies bore witness to a "wind-down of a period of incredibly dense change and development in art," a period of creative lull where innovation in art was "at a halt."[4] Nuttall was not alone in his pessimism. In the early 1970s, B.S. Johnson wrote of his despair at the static form of the British novel, which was plotted, and which plodded on, as though

James Joyce had never existed.[5] Around the same time, Nuttall wrote of his "enormous determination to arrive at some point of literary structure as multi-levelled and self-perpetuating as *Finnegans Wake*," concluding, like Johnson, that it was "a monument past which subsequent innovators have failed to go."[6]

Nuttall had been at the forefront of what became a global underground movement. Between 1963 and 1967, he edited *My Own Mag: A Super Absorbant [sic] Periodical*, which used "nausea and flagrant scatology as violent means of presentation."[7] Against the odds, by the fifth issue, Nuttall's experimental mimeographed magazine became the preeminent forum for avant-garde writing across the globe. British writers, including B. S. Johnson, sent in their work ("Coleridge hated Cologne; I have been to Cologne and I hate Coleridge"); German avant-garde writers experimented with cut-ups (Carl Weissner) and a host of Beat writers and fellow voyagers tried out new forms, among them Robert Creeley, Allen Ginsberg and William Burroughs.[8] "The web was connecting up its separate strands," Nuttall recalled. "Something was clearly happening."[9]

Despite his pivotal role in the development of avant-garde artistic production during the 1960s, Nuttall remains an elusive figure. While his output was prodigious, Nuttall's refusal to concentrate on one or other artistic form has led to an uncertain legacy, at least in the history of mainstream post-war British culture. As a poet, painter, illustrator, critic, essayist, biographer, actor, performance artist and editor, Nuttall's vast body of work, like that of his own unapologetically corpulent frame, refused to be straight-jacketed. During the 1960s, Nuttall was instrumental in developing *The People Show*, Britain's longest running experimental theatre group. As a poet, Nuttall achieved recognition with what he called the "lyric impressionist vein" of his verse; his work was showcased, along with the Scottish poet Alan Jackson and William Wantling, the American poet laureate of San Quentin Prison, in the prestigious Penguin Modern Poets series.[10] Nuttall's fiction, on the other hand, has all but gone unnoticed; his dozen or so novellas and novelettes are out of print.[11] In sharp contrast to his close contemporary and occasional collaborator, B.S. Johnson, whose avant-garde writing has been reissued and repackaged, Nuttall's fiction, including *Come Back Sweet Prince: A Novelette* (1966) and *The Foxes Lair* (1972) remains the provenance of second hand book dealers. While Nuttall published several conventionally presented hard-bound prose works, including *The Gold Hole* (1978), a number of them were published as limited edition pamphlets, including *The Anatomy of My Father's Corpse* (1975) a meditation on the death of his father, and the short illustrated story *Oscar Christ and the Immaculate Conception* (1970), the tale of a German police chief who is accused of arranging the murder of his girlfriend.

While the lack of availability of Nuttall's novellas may in part account for the scant recognition he has received as a writer of avant-garde fiction, his novellas, replete with violent and sexual imagery, were at odds with what he termed the prevailing "dictatorial criticism" which continued to champion the retrograde "seemly literature" of social realism.[12] While Bob Dylan sang of times-a-changing, the British novel retreated indoors, away from the hard rain of change, where it continued to nurture character and plot. Like Nuttall, who drew attention to the chaos and fragility of contemporary cold war life, B.S. Johnson, writing in the introduction to *Aren't You Rather Young to be Writing Your Memoirs?* (1973), insisted that "Life does not tell stories. Life is chaotic, fluid, random; it leaves myriads of ends untied, untidily," a clear dig at contemporary British fiction, which was still propped up by the "crutch of storytelling." As Johnson observed, "Nathalie Sarraute once described literature as a relay race, the baton of innovation passing from one generation to another. The vast majority of British novelists has dropped the baton, stood still, turned back, or not even realised that there is a race."[13]

While Nuttall was garnering praise from counter-cultural royalty, novelist-critics were defending themselves against the onslaught of experimental fiction, a term Johnson and others deplored. In the preface to *Pig* (1969), a sequence of prose-poetry cut-ups, Burroughs declared that the Nuttall "is one of the few writers today who actually handles his medium," while David Lodge would dismiss the author of *The Naked Lunch* as nothing "more than a minor eccentric figure."[14] Lodge's essay, 'Objections to William Burroughs', was more than a parting shot at the American author: "Have we come to handle the *avant-garde* too gently?", he begins his essay, in which he implicitly incriminates authors of the British experimental novel, among them Johnson, Ann Quin and Brigid Brophy, writers who practised divergent techniques, but who were frequently lumped together.[15] For the likes of C. P. Snow and Kingsley Amis, avant-garde fiction was an assault on the British novel, illustrated by their fiercely fought campaign to "run experimental writing out of town"—and presumably back across the Atlantic, illustrated by two special issues on the avant-garde in the *Times Literary Supplement*, both in 1963 which were dominated by U.S. writers.[16]

Nuttall's fictional writing emerged from within and around these debates. *The Case of Isabel and the Bleeding Foetus*, his first substantial novella, was published in 1967. Characteristic of many of his works, the book is a collage of poems, transcriptions and diary entries which morph from one section to another, just as Nuttall's prose frequently bleeds into poetry, a feature of his writing that he acknowledges in *The Anatomy of My Father's Corpse*. There he notes his "determination not write this down in verse," but rather to "put this in prose that the wonder of it might not be that flexing copper irony of pain . . ."[17]

The Case of Isabel introduces a number of recurrent themes in Nuttall's fiction, which is frequently scatological, sexual and disturbing. The Holy Ghost is reconceived as the Phallic Ghost; there is an unexplained "crumpled weeping foetus," a recurring motif in Nuttall's work, described "with an egghead of blood and a fleshknot of a face from whose screwed-up cuntformation eyes the tears of blood splash . . ."[18] Prenatal, yet able to cry, the foetus, with its unformed bloody features, "leaves the assaulted senses uncertain," as Nuttall describes an installation by Herman Nitsch, "whether dead flesh is alive, live dead, or whether, and here is the message, there is any difference."[19] As Emily Beber observes, Nuttall "was drawn to the body for its lack of control, for its unwillingness to give into the sensory rationalising that was taking place; as much as the voices of authority might try to mechanise them, their permeation would remain skin deep, the body still able to involuntary erupt . . ."[20] While British experimental writers were putting their necks on the line, Nuttall was putting out a great deal more as he explored the boundaries between text, body and art. At a happening in the mid-1960s, Nuttall recalls how he fitted himself out as a sculpture, hiding "behind a screen and just had my belly and my prick and one finger coming through holes," in what became a striking example of art, not imitating, life, but becoming it.[21]

Nuttall's willingness to put himself on show, to erode the boundaries between sculptor and sculpture, is a fitting metaphor for his Rabelaisian work where the body is frequently on display, unclothed, fleshy and sexually voracious. Heavily influenced by Sade, Bataille, Artaud and Burroughs, Nuttall's work explores and develops what he called "the aesthetic of obscenity" as a way to "force people to accept life and live it"—an outlook that he is careful to distinguish from the "obscenity" of *The Naked Lunch,* which was "intended as a device for obliterating life as it had ever been known."[22] This tension between an impulse to destroy, and the impulse to "accept life and live it" is played out poignantly by his novella *Snipe's Spinster* (1975), a work in which Nuttall explores, but never quite resolves, his political and aesthetic radicalism.

For Calder and Boyars, a leading publisher of American and European avant-garde writing, including works by Burroughs and John Cage, *Snipe's Spinster* is "an important book, not only for the clear picture it gives us of the time in which we are living, but for the possibilities it opens for the novel," adding that Nuttall "has given the novel a whole new voice to work with."[23] Despite the energetic affirmations on the dust-jacket, *Snipe's Spinster* is not immediately obvious as a work of avant-garde or experimental fiction. Aside from the book's cover, a sketch of two men drawn by Nuttall, one with a gun that fires a drooping flower, there are no illustrations, and the novel flirts with social realism. The story, which is indebted to cold war spy thrillers such as Richard Condon's *The Manchurian Candidate,* is narrated by the eponymous Snipe, a jazz musician and jaded revolutionary who resolves to assassinate the "Man", an anonymous world power figure. The novel ends with Snipe hiding behind a hayrick as he loads his gun, but in contrast to *The Gold Hole*, which contains interlocking stories of abortion and child murders, the gun is not fired, and the assassination does not take place. *Snipe's Spinster*, the publishers note, is Nuttall's "attempt to kiss goodbye to *Bomb Culture* as a book by which to be identified," but the image of the unfired gun suggests that there is no resolution to the revolution of the 1960s, a theme which dominates *Snipe's Spinster*.[24]

Despite Nuttall's assertion that he envisaged writing *Snipe's Spinster* as a means of distancing himself from *Bomb Culture*, the two books are bear striking similarities. Like *Bomb Culture*, *Snipe's Spinster* contains careful scholarly notes on works culled from key counter-cultural figures, many of whom are discussed in his earlier book, including Gregory Corso, Allen Ginsberg, Bob Dylan and Lenny Bruce. Indeed, the cacophony of counter-cultural voices produces a disorientating effect on both the reader and narrator whose tale documents "why that revolution failed."[25] Old revolutionary stalwarts like McGregor ("Black donkey jacket . . . Woolly bear and one ear-ring") persist with "self-indulgent marching" while faddish insurgents like Tippet, "whose first self-appointed job was playing guitar in the office of *International Times*, "has donned and discarded terms like hippie, Yippie, White Panther . . . as fast as the changing hang of his jeans."[26] Snipe himself is kept in check by his "spinster", a Jiminy Cricket moral conscience, "a bore and virgin", who learns not to goad me into ambitious moral decisions."[27]

As the novel concludes, Snipe, conscious that he may be shot by the Secret Service men who guard the "Man", writes a letter to his lover Lindy, which is part explanation for his deed, and part moral and political manifesto. Central to Snipe's belief is that a few powerful corrupt men have impoverished the world by threatening energy, a form of sinister control that "fatigues", which in turn stifles radicalism and nullifies radical art. The shock induced by watching the self-mutilation of the performance artist Otto Muehl during the 1960s, Nuttall contends, is lost a decade later "now that brutality had been rendered so broadly stylish and commonplace."[28] In Nuttall's 1970s hell, a purgatory between 1960s radical potential and the second coming of the revolution, culture has become dissipated, illustrated by his reference to the Second Law of Thermodynamics in his letter to Lindy. Like Thomas Pynchon in his short story 'Entropy', and like John Barth's 'Literature of Exhaustion', Nuttall pictures the horror of a world without revolutionary aesthetic energy, a monoculture sold by the "Man" and bought by us all.[29]

Half-drunk, and without a coherent plan, it seems likely that Snipe will fail to kill the "Man". Inevitably, it seems, the revolutionary energy will dissipate. And yet this is not quite so. In two quiet moments in the novel, away from the tumult of the myriad counter-cultural voices, Nuttall explores the redemptive energy of grace, a term not usually associated with revolution or radicalism. At the start of the novella, Snipe finds "grace" in Lindy's body; he finds in her limbs an "authentic grace precisely because they know no system."[30] Later, as he writes his final letter, he marvels at the grace of Lindy's mind and soul, observing how these "ideas and impulses . . . cross and re-cross . . . without them once getting knotted."[31] Unfettered by structure and unburdened by experience, grace, Nuttall suggests—in a description that might be applied to his own fiction—is truly revolutionary: "It is the quintessence of energy, you see, energy's highest form, more marvellous than lightning or the sun because it's actually useful and it's wondrously absurd."[32]

Endnotes

1 Jeff Nuttall, *Bomb Culture* (London: Paladin, 1968) 146.

2 *Ibid.,* 19, 58, 141.

3 Jeff Nuttall, *Snipe's Spinster* (London: Calder and Boyars, 1975); Jonathan Green, *Days in the Life: Voices from the English Underground, 1961-1971* (London: Minerva, 1989), 271.

4 Jeff Nuttall, 'Introduction', *The House Party* (Toronto: Basilike, 1975), no pagination.

5 See B. S. Johnson, 'Introduction', *Aren't You Rather Young to be Writing Your Memoirs* (1973) http://bsjohnson.co.uk/2015/02/introduction-from-arent-you-rather-young-to-be-writing-your-memoirs-1973

6 Nuttall, 'Introduction', *The House Party,* no pagination.

7 Nuttall, *Bomb Culture,* 141.

8 B.S. Johnson, *My Own Mag,* 6 (July 1964). Weissner's work appears in issues 12, 13, 14 and 17; Creely's and Ginsberg's in issue 9; Burroughs became a key contributor. His cut-ups appear in issues 2, 4, 5, 6, 7, 8, 9, 11, 12, 13 and 15. See Reality Studio http://realitystudio.org/bibliographic-bunker/my-own-mag/my-own-mag-index-of-names/ for an index of contributors, as well as scanned copies of the complete run of *My Own Mag.*

9 Nuttall, *Bomb Culture,* 159.

10 Nuttall, *Performance Art: Memoirs, Volume 1* (London: Calder, 1979), 132. Nuttall, Wantling and Jackson appear together in *Penguin Modern Poets,* volume 12, published in 1968.

11 I am indebted to Jay Jeff Jones for pointing out that *Muscle* was Nuttall's 11th novella but there is also an unlisted work of fiction, *Teeth.* In addition, Nuttall composed "Telephone Novels", which were composed on the spot with the public.

12 Nuttall, *Bomb Culture,* 54.

13 Johnson, 'Introduction', *Aren't You Rather Young to be Writing Your Memoirs* (1973) http://bsjohnson.co.uk/2015/02/introduction-from-arent-you-rather-young-to-be-writing-your-memoirs-1973/

14 William Burroughs, 'Preface', *Pig* (London: Fulcrum Press, 1969), no pagination; David Lodge, 'Objections to William Burroughs', *Critical Quarterly* 8, 3 (September 1966): 205.

15 Lodge, 'Objections to William Burroughs': 203.

16 Francis Booth, *Amongst Those Left: The British Experimental Novel, 1940-1980* (lulu.com, 2012), 31. See, John Willet, 'The Changing Guard', *Times Literary Supplement* (6 August 1964), 675. Americans mentioned included Allen Ginsberg, the artist Robert Watts and William Burroughs. British artists include the concrete poet Dom (Pierre-) Sylvester Houédard and the playwright John Arden. See also Willet, 'The Changing Guard II', *Times Literary Supplement* (3 September 1964), 775.

17 Jeff Nuttall, *The Anatomy of My Father's Corpse* (Toronto: Basilike, 1975), 1. Edition limited to 675 copies.

18 Jeff Nuttall, *The Case of Isobel and the Bleeding Foetus* (London: Turret, 1967), 12.

19 Nuttall, *Snipe's Spinster,* 106.

20 Emily Beber, 'Jeff Nuttall's *My Own Mag*', forthcoming.

21 Green, *Days in the Life*, 59.

22 Nuttall, *Bomb Culture,* 142.

23 Dust-jacket of *Snipe's Spinster*.

24 *Ibid.*

25 Nuttall, *Snipe's Spinster*, 59.

26 *Ibid.*, 60, 103, 89, 90.

27 *Ibid.*, 12.

28 *Ibid.*, 114, 110.

29 'Entropy' was first published in 1960; it is reprinted in Thomas Pynchon, *Slow Learner: Early Stories* (London: Vintage, 2000). Barth's essay was first published in 1967 and it is reprinted in *The Friday Book: Essays and Other Nonfiction* (London and Baltimore: Johns Hopkins University Press, 1984).

30 Nuttall, *Snipe's Spinster*, 31.

31 *Ibid.*, 113.

32 *Ibid.*, 113.

Nine Digressions on Narrative Authority

RONALD SUKENICK

I. The Politics of Authority

When we talk about "reality" with regard to fiction, what we're really talking about is the authority to comment plausibly on experience. The concept of "realism" in fiction is notoriously literary; that is, it depends on a set of rules for composition, now conventional, and understood all too well by a reader even superficially educated in our literary tradition who can acquiesce to them without the least thought, as if he were reading a newspaper. But the novel at least, without considering other forms of fiction, is distinguished, "realistic" or not, by its claim on a consensual reality, and has even functioned as a major medium of transition between experience—with all its implications of personalism, subjectivity, and, at the limit, solipsism—and "reality" which, "as everybody knows, is precisely that which everybody knows." A word must be said immediately for that subjectivity which the novel, from one point of view, is always striving to escape. It is just that subjectivity, that sense of individual experience, that is most threatened by media, propaganda, cliché and the "literary", by which I mean writing that depends too much on the accumulating "text" of the culture. Yes, culture, if not experience, can be considered as an ever-expanding text. Why not? But in fact life is not a book, not even cultural life, and any consideration of what gives prestige and authority to a text—appeals to tradition, "taste" and other mysteries of expertise notwithstanding—

without accounting for questions of social class, economics, the politics of culture and pure accident is, to reinstitute a term popular in the sixties, phony. The establishment, of course, is always eager to profit from an illusion of "standards" based on the clichés of consumer manipulation and the static effect of tradition at the expense of individual experience. This is to say, simply, that literature is not the sanction for literature. Personally, I'm quite certain there is an argument to be made in justification of literature on a purely formal basis, but it probably would have more to do with neurology than literary tradition, which is too compromised by history to provide criteria not contingent on other areas of experience. So, from another point of view, we can consider the novel as an instrument that undercuts official versions of reality in favor of our individual sense of experience, now constantly threatened by the brain wash of politics and the mass market. Deviations from the latter in the direction of individual experience are labelled "narcissistic," "self-indulgent" and "pretentious." Marketing reduces tradition itself to slogans and nostalgia, compelling intellectuals to consider seriously such alternatives as "pop" and "camp." These are ploys which are illuminating insofar as they invert and therefore demystify "elitist" literary taste, but turning the dialogue upside down does not necessarily advance it. In any case, it's difficult to say which is more egregiously literary these days, the popular philosophy of the highbrow novel ne'er so well expressed, or the commercial imitators of a prior mode of realistic imitation whose practice is curiously in line with the recommendations of John Barth's view, before recent revision, that literature should imitate literature. This situation comes at the very moment, naturally, when no particular source of literary authority has any commanding intellectual sanction. The "literary establishment" is a notion that has become ambiguously literary as it becomes increasingly commercialized. Of the traditional alternatives, the avant-garde, in its ceaseless search for the new, has ceased to be importantly different, the "underground" was merchandised away by the sixties, and the "experimental" is a meaningless label. The literary elite, including the best critical minds, has moved to the university where practical criticism is often considered unworthy, a form of journalism, and many theorists are heavily involved in a new form of belles-lettres, encroaching on, rather than evaluating activity in the traditional genres. The matter of criteria in fiction has been left largely to the economics of the publishing industry which increasingly require formula commercial fiction, and the cultural sorties of the New Right, the only coherent group in view to grasp and exploit the connections among art, authority, and politics.

II. Realism

There is no contemporary Novel. The contemporary situation is rather that different kinds of novels may serve different purposes. The authority of the realistic/naturalistic mode is too deeply embedded in our tradition to lose its utility for fiction. There are persuasive reasons today for writing fiction in the realistic forms, even though such writing in no way represents "the state of the art." Realism, for example, can be useful during the emergence of a minority or oppressed culture into increased consciousness. It can provide a means for the presentation and evaluation of the data important to the life of a cultural group when it most needs to hold the mirror up to itself and its surrounding milieu. Naturalism may be especially useful to the phase when a subculture is beginning to take stock of what it's all about and how it relates to other parts of its world because of naturalism's cataloguing function; moreover, there is the fatalistic aspect of the naturalistic novel which clarifies the relation of the individual to the necessities of industrial society. The *Studs Lonigan* series, though stylistically an artifact from late nineteenth-century European fiction, was nevertheless appropriate to Irish-American culture of the thirties. This kind of novel persuades because it embodies the data of the culture as perceived by its members, and the narrative point of view will go unchallenged because it has the authority of their knowledge. But what happens to such narrative authority when the data of a culture become ambiguous? The status of the narrator must reflect the conditions of the historical moment or suffer a loss of credibility. In Jane Bowles' *Two Serious Ladies*, for example, a novel that evokes a certain cultural aimlessness and loss of certitude, we have a narrative voice we can trust, but—or even because—there is a kind of intentional feathering off into the unknown and the ambiguous. This voice comprises a form of omniscient narration that, if not actually influenced by Kafka (which is neither here nor there) must be looked at in view of Kafka. That is, in Kafka we have omniscient narration, but it's omniscient narration in which part of the omniscience is, paradoxically, awareness of its limits. The normal situation of the omniscient narrator is inverted. What the narrative voice knows is the extent of the unknown. This may be omniscient narration technically, but intellectually, spiritually, it is the reverse of the Victorian voice of authority which implies that everything, if not known, is at least knowable. In Kafka, the narrative voice implies that you may think you know quite a bit but in fact you know very little and the more you look at things the less knowable they are until, finally, there is very little, if anything, you know at all. Realism, insofar as it is a component of Kafka's style, retains its authority only through its admission that reality is unknowable. The narrative situation there is not totally unlike the effect of the flood of information in a Pynchon novel, which by its very excess becomes finally ambiguous. If we admit the authority of Kafka's example, it conditions the use of the realistic form in a terminal way. There are, of course, levels in the culture where the rules may be clear and the essentials of the locale knowable—a regional or heavily class-defined setting, enclaves like the academic world, the homosexual world—and where the authority of the narrator's knowledge may go unquestioned. But one might risk the generalization that at present the authority of the realistic form is a self-conscious one, including an awareness of its limits as well as of its alternatives. *The French Lieutenant's Woman* would be a case in point. Another would be Rudolfo Anaya's *Bless Me Ultima*, whose incorporation of the magical from the Chicano tradition into the style of what might be called "anglo-realism," expands the limits of the latter in the direction of Latin

American "Magic Realism."

III. Fragmentation

In *The Sound and the Fury* and *As I Lay Dying* the authority of realism is retained in a contingent way by establishing a narrative situation in which it appears that the truth may be arrived at through comparison of different, fragmented versions. This is, after all, one of our normal and accepted ways of arriving at truth, as in the testimony of witnesses in court, and is immediately persuasive at the level of common sense. It enters our literary tradition most obviously in the transition from, say, Edith Wharton to Henry James, or from early to late James. The persuasiveness of the contingent explains why a super-conscious writer like James would claim that a certain amount of stupidity is necessary in writing a good novel, a claim that complements the Jamesian strategy of reader obfuscation. The drive toward ambiguity in James and Conrad is not so far from Gide's techniques in *The Counterfeiters* to impede any tendency to assume a naive version of reality, or even from Viktor Shklovsky's doctrine of "retardation," which has a similar effect. In Conrad a story is typically told through the incorporation—in the form itself—of the situation of limited narrative knowledge, implying that the reader not only cannot but should not trust a voice of total authority. Conrad's storytellers within the story constitute a re-framing of the story from the point of view of contingency, because it is the contingent that is persuasive. In a book like Tom Glynn's novel, *Temporary Sanity*, the breakdown of narrative authority takes a peculiar democratic turn, in which the idea seems to be to investigate the populist mind and its limitations. The result is a book one of whose virtues is the description of how things seem from the point of view of stupidity, which creates another kind of contingent narrative authority. The narrative situation is similar in Michael Brownstein's persuasively lunatic *Country Cousins* and—but in terms of middle class blandness—in the fiction of James Schuyler. The area of authority for realism may have moved from description of social reality to description of points of view about it. Nabokov's eccentric narrative stances disclose not a common reality but the power of the imagination to affect it.

IV. *The Reflexive*

A quasi-religious mode that retains a certain amount of authority is that of testimony, or confession. If the novelist as god-the-father is no longer persuasive, a subjective or diaristic account of one's own experience would seem to be a rhetorically acceptable stance. That the mode crystallized by Henry Miller, however, now yields limited if attractive *tours de faiblesse* on the order of *Catcher in the Rye*, Frank Conroy's *Stoptime*, or, more recently, Jim Carroll's *The Basketball Diaries*, is no doubt indicative of our more sophisticated consciousness of the limits of language. Awareness of language as a coherent reality in itself, that both impedes and facilitates our description of experience, as—in the now familiar comparison—the instruments used in atomic physics interfere with the observation they make possible, quickly engenders a self-consciousness in the confessional mode, a consciousness, that is, of the effects of the instrument of observation. The consciousness that literature both reveals and falsifies experience is incorporated in the formal irony of fiction in the "death of the novel" or "literature of exhaustion" period at the end of the sixties. In the hands of a super-conscious writer like Peter Handke, the confessional carries an awareness not only of the limits of that particular form of narration, but of the limits of language itself, so that the only way to retain the authority of the text is to incorporate that awareness of it. The narration then must turn back on itself. The reflexive texts of Genet and Beckett had already established textual self-reference as a condition of authenticity in the fifties. Their example has long since been taken into account by writers like Jonathan Baumbach, Walter Abish, Clarence Major and, in fact, almost every fiction writer working with the state of the art and, consequently, at the limits of the fictive imagination.

V. The Collective Voice

By the end of the sixties self-consciousness in terms of form became unavoidable, involving, as it did, the general sense of the limits of language and of the process of narration itself. One reaction to the personalism of the confessional mode, as well as to the apparent abstraction of the reflexive, was a move toward the authority of the collective voice. What I would call pseudo-mythology was a step toward such an alternative. This was an interest shared by such writers as Robert Coover, Steve Katz, John Barth, and William Gass, and was a trend parallel to that of the pseudo-autobiography utilized by some of the novelists writing in an apparently confessional mode that was in fact an imitation of that mode, like the "true histories" of the eighteenth century. A problem with myth, however, is that it's antihistorical, so that what is gained in authority by retelling traditional stories of one sort or another may be lost in the sense that they are "only stories." Once a myth is recognized as such, its fictive component is emphasized and its lack of innocence becomes obvious. Among the more fruitful influences in this area was that of the Latin American novelists in their use of a collective voice. I take it that the South Americans had antecedents in an important North American voice, Faulkner, who, however influenced by Joyce, is very different from him in that his collective voice is not that of "the tradition." In the Americas, where we work without a tradition comparable to that of Europe—where it might even be said that we have a basically antitraditional attitude—the resort to a collective voice will inevitably have a very distinctive character, neither mythic nor traditional, but a common voice credible in terms of experience as against the manipulative claims of pop, populist, or mass market ideologies. That is the authority one senses, for example, in Jean Toomer's *Cane*, at those moments when the experience of the rural South overwhelms the voice of the urban black and begins to speak through him. And that is why the essentially solipsistic form of *One Hundred Years of Solitude* is perfect: Macondo is precisely not history, however much of the historical it may include, but a construction of the way people believe themselves to be. Books in this Faulknerian mode tend to be oracular because a people's version of itself, not in bondage to history, has the power to affect the future. In Gilbert Sorrentino's *Mulligan Stew*, on the other hand, you get the Joycean situation of the use of epic, traditional reference by means of which contemporary experience is amplified and put in context. Sorrentino's novel, through Joyce and Flann O'Brien, uses the authority of the epic tradition specifically and the cultural tradition in general. It is a book which, in the epic manner, intends a certain scope, though its style is mock epic, resulting in an oddly modest exercise despite its sprawl. *Ulysses* and *Finnegans Wake* have the dimensions of an attempt at cultural summation that makes Mulligan look like a local joke in the mode of *The Rape of the Lock*. But there is something moving in the attempt, especially in the way this innovative book only makes sense toward the end where it is most deeply embedded in the past. It is a formally untraditional novel whose only rationale is in the tradition it mocks, a tradition, moreover, that is extremely remote from the American present. Its synthesis, though it does not ring false, is cameo in all but size, limiting the contemporary authority of the narrative voice in order to invoke that of the past. An interesting, if much less successful, effort to establish a persuasive narrative point of view is Robert Nichols' recent utopian tetralogy, *Daily Lives in Nghsi-Altai*, which attempts to resurrect the omniscient voice through the authority of the sociopolitical collective. However, its tone of utopian irony ("wouldn't it be nice if it were so?") suggests a consciousness that cultural authority cannot be established by social fiat.

VI. The Autonomous Text

The reflexive text gives up the idea, finally, of a voice of authority speaking *through* the book. Textual self-reference makes it clear that authority can only reside in the text itself. Richard Brautigan has fun with the situation in a style that acknowledges the reality of the text as opposed to the reality of its subject. In Donald Barthelme's *The Dead Father*, there is no "big picture" to which the text can refer as its authority. In fact, that novel represents an attempt to move beyond the fragments in which Barthelme usually deals toward some form of synthesis, an attempt to reestablish the authority that died with the paternal force. As the novel tells us, the older generation is interested in the big picture, but the younger generation knows there is no big picture and therefore it's more interested in the frame. *The Dead Father* is an attempt to impose a frame on the chaos of experience in order to make sense of it. But if there is no "big picture" there can be no authoritative frame, and we are left with a novel in which the fragments are more powerful than the synthesis. With the loss of the frame and the authority of the frame, which is to say, the authority of the narrative, there comes a loss of the authority of the narrator, and at that phase one begins to hear not only about the death of the novel but also about the death of the author. The author who, failing all else, was presumed to be the source and guarantor of the integrity of the text, turns out to have no such authority. The author becomes someone who, you might say, activates the process of language through the system of a given text, allowing the language to speak itself. Kenneth Gangemi's *Olt*, for example, represents an effective annihilation of the author in favor of the autonomy of found fragments. In the "constrictive" texts of the Oulipo group (Queneau, Calvino, Perec, Harry Matthews, among others) the writer's essential role is to formulate a rule or rules from which the text systematically unfolds —Perec's omission of the letter *e* from his novel *La Disparition*. The text is a preprogrammed system that generates itself. A related example is Burrough's manipulation of fragments in the cut-up method, heightening the reality of the text as a generative medium. In Daniel Spoerri's *An Anecdotal Topography of Chance*, the text is autonomous in that it is a system activated in particular ways depending on how the reader chooses to read it. To a certain extent, this is also true of Cortazar's *Hopscotch*.

VII. Docutext

A logical extension of the decreased importance of the narrator, and even of the author, is the kind of documentary text that we get in the books of Michael Ondaatje and Paul Metcalf. This technique derives its authority from actual use of the data, texts, and testimonies of the culture. It is a strategy that plays with what we consider to be the source of truth in the culture insofar as we acknowledge one at all, the truth of empirical observation. There are all sorts of variants of the documentary novel: faction, the nonfiction novel, the works of Tom Wolfe, Hunter Thompson, Doctorow, Mailer, and Capote. However, even given that there is always a certain amount of imagination in journalism and a certain amount of subjective interference in works supposedly based on empirical observation, the use of those forms in basically fictive integrations denies them the only kind of authority particular to them. The work of Metcalf and Ondaatje, as well as that of Burroughs, is more persuasive, in that it deals not with presumed "fact" but with manipulation of received texts. They leave the ambiguities of fact and observation to others and deal directly with language itself. This mode avoids the drawback of the novel of information of which Pynchon is the master, whose authority depends on the very American credulity about accumulation of data, as if truth and quantity are necessarily identical. The docutext also avoids or, at least, evades the mysteries of subjectivity that seem to terrify many American novelists, even though it might be argued that an investigation of consciousness is precisely the direction in which one must move when the sanctions for observation become ambiguous. In Metcalf, risks are limited by limiting the narrative situation to an ironic one in which collaged texts are left to comment on one another. The gain is in finding an apparent way to move beyond the reflexive, though it could be argued that what is sacrificed here is the original referent for the sake of a new linguistic integration twice removed from the data on which it is based.

Various other ways of moving out of the cul-de-sac of self-reference developed in the sixties and seventies. Burroughs' cut-up method, through collage, releases information in his materials that is unpremeditated and not manufactured by his own ego. Another method involves a kind of imprinting of phenomena in the manner of the sculptor Keinholz, or of Se-gal's plaster-casting of his models. Photo- or hyper-realism, however, like the *nouveau roman*, has its limits as statement. That the surface of the subject can never be reproduced by the surface of the composition about it, however "realistic," is a one-shot insight that cannot maintain the foreground long without referring—if not to the original subject—then to a contextual background developed by the composition. If the surface represents images from common experience, the background represents their metamorphosis by consciousness through language. In *The Death of the Novel and Other Stories*, I attempted, with intentional naivete, a new realism by taking imprints of "reality" with a tape recorder with varying combinations of such foreground/background relations in order to move beyond the impasse of narrative authority implied by the general increase in our consciousness of linguistic and narrative limitations. In fact, the variety and sophistication of the actual narrative attempts to meet this situation—as opposed to theories about it—thrives in the United States, not to mention the Americas, with a vigor unmatched by parallel developments in Europe. One of the components of so-called postmodernism is simply a move away from European models for narrative. On the other hand, our practical criticism lags behind developments in fiction, often seeming stubbornly simpleminded. Think of "moral fiction".

VIII. Process Text

One consequence of the breakdown of the narrative frame is to throw into question the matter of how a narrative should begin and end. A work of fiction, rather than being defined by the traditional beginning-middle-end kind of closure, might under the circumstances be considered as a process whose beginning and end are incidental rather than intrinsic to its form, and whose distinctive feature is the way it unfolds. Its continuity rather than its closure would define it. Such a work might, for example, take the form of a series, theme and variations, or systematized proliferation, any of which could end at any point after its essential mode had been established without fundamentally altering its character. A process text derives its authority in part by being able to acknowledge the reality of the processes of writing and reading beyond artifice, a narrative situation that is approached in, for example, *Malone Dies*. John Barth's well-known story, "A Self Recorded Fiction," is a witty and accurate parody of the text as a self-referential process. However, it seems to be based on the assumption that the basic authority for fiction is imitation of reality, which, once called into question, can only result in the text turning back on itself in the form of reflexive parody. Barth's response to this impasse is an admission and attempted exploitation of the situation, found in his essay "The Literature of Exhaustion," which in effect recommends that literature turn from imitation of reality to imitation of literature. This attempt to turn defeat into victory is based on an initial misapprehension of defeat. Fiction does not and cannot have the same sanctions as history or journalism. Critics who attack contemporary fiction for "self-consciousness" are really attacking its momentum toward increased consciousness of narrative as a medium. Increased consciousness provokes anxiety, but nevertheless that look in the mirror is part of the culture's impulse toward an increasingly intelligent proliferation of its own existence, part of our ongoing process of civilization. We not only need to know things, we also need to know that we know them and how we know them, questions of authority that contemporary fiction takes into account as do philosophy, science, linguistics, sociology, and other disciplines. If we admit the validity of an ongoing process of cultural creation, it would seem that the creative processes we have devised to that end have a certain validity in themselves. We can say then that the job of narrative fiction is not to record some preexisting reality but to contribute to the ongoing process of culture building in and through the process of writing itself. The act of narrative creation then assumes a fundamental authority more or less embodied by particular examples, some of which expose the essentials of process itself, as in the works of Genet, or Raymond Federman.

IX. *The Holy Book*

Narrative fiction, unlike history or journalism, is about what hasn't happened. Like religion, though in a different way, it deals in faith. For the believer, "once upon a time" means, "here is something that hasn't happened, but might." Fiction may falsify the past but it helps invent the future. In fact, formally, all stories lead us into the future, into what is going to happen. Narrative, by its very nature, is a process of what happens next, and next, and next. Every novel is in the nature of prophecy in that it represents the projection of a future. But the essential trope of fiction is hypothesis, provisional supposition, a technique that requires suspension of belief as well as of disbelief. Thus, if fiction deals in faith, it also deals in skepticism, requiring the point of view of both Sancho and Quijote. We have to take the projections of fiction, finally, on faith, but on faith tested by the challenges of experience. If the sacred can be defined as faith in a particular course of events, as in our holy books, it might be said that fiction turns the profane into the sacred in a process whose authority derives from the continuous skeptical challenges of common experience. So regarded, fiction might disclose the potential for certain functions and rhetorical possibilities long neglected by its European tradition and not to be found in the recent dominant examples of Hemingway and Fitzgerald. The flow of experience can never be framed —it passes and is gone. But the artifacts that art produces exist in an eddy of experience where they can be reexperienced, contemplated and re-visioned in the context of the reflexive mirrorings and reduplications of meditative consciousness. Repetition is an essential of literary art, from the pure repetition of metric in poetry to the re-creation and contemplation of experience that is fundamental to fiction. The incremental repetitions and re-visions of literary writing signify its existence in a realm continuous with the common flow of experience, but reflexively intensified, one that can avail itself of special forms and a special language.

Perhaps the authority of narrative writing at this point might profit from drawing on the powers of high rhetoric, of, for example, the Sublime, and on narrative effects ignored by our tradition of mimesis. Such techniques can summon up the intense affect required for the emotional integrations and disintegrations associated with matters of faith rather than with those of description and reportage. In moving into areas associated with the sacred text, such as parable, prayer, incantation, magic, prophecy, and myth of origin, in becoming a medium between individual and collective experience opposing the manipulations of the media, a medium that might serve as an oracular bridge to reconnect the profane with a sense of the sacred, the narrative might once more authenticate fiction as having some urgency other than the commercial. This is certainly one of the directions indicated in Joyce, especially in *Finnegans Wake*. But along with the repetitions of tradition in Joyce goes a corresponding iconoclasm, a profanation and dismemberment of tradition through collage. Collage is a technique for cutting up received texts in order to examine the possibility of new integrations, and so serves as a method for desacralization. Profanity, blasphemy, and desecration perform dark and necessary services in the holy book, moralists notwithstanding. They have the power, not to forge the uncreated conscience of the race, but to help uncreate the forged consciousness of the mass market, the mass media, the masses, or of whatever forces serve as mystification of the course of experience. The skepticism consequential to suspension of belief opens dangerous possibilities of change in belief. In places where art is taken seriously—Eastern Europe, France, Latin America, China, almost everywhere but in the Anglo-American tradition—artists have inherent political status because they are perceived as dealing with belief. The Anglo-American doctrine of willing suspension of disbelief neuters our narrative writing and confirms its inferiority and bondage to fact rather than its liberation in thought. Fiction has to lay claim to truth beyond that of data if it is to reinstate its authority in competition with the prestige of journalism and the high-flown journalism of mimesis. Journalism and history are oriented toward the present and past. It may be that the claim of fiction, incorporating as it does our attempt to reconcile our hopes with our fate, is on the future.

From *In Form: Digressions on the Act of Fiction*, 1985, Southern Illinois University. Reprinted with permission.

Never Never Again

DOUG NUFER

It occurred to me to write a novel where no word could be used more than once. This was around 1990, after I'd finished my first constraint-driven novel, *Negativeland*, and three years after I met Harry Mathews and Jacques Roubaud of Oulipo and learned about that group of Paris-based writers and mathematicians, who came up with constraints for writing poetry and prose.

In *Negativeland*, every sentence has a negative and the plot simultaneously runs forwards and backwards. To distract myself from the business of trying to get that book published, I aimed to take on a project that was so overwhelmingly difficult, any secondary goal, such as publication, would be superfluous. I looked for an unprecedented constraint that was hard to do and easy to check, such as Georges Perec writing the novel *La Disparition* (*A Void*) without the letter e. And while I intended to disrupt the conventions of the novel, I had to follow those conventions. Anybody could write 200 pages of lines where no word appeared more than once and call it a novel, poem, index, or whatever; I wanted to make a story.

I began with the comforting assurance that a sentence consists of a noun and a verb. However prepositions, articles, and conjunctions make sentences flow smoothly, these little words are inessential to grammar. The British novelist Henry Green, who was hard of hearing, wrote perfectly tuned prose by often omitting these bit parts of speech. I also began with an opening that had been languishing in one manuscript or another, from my years of writing unconstrained prose: "When the racetrack closed forever, I had to get a job." With "a", "the", "to", and "I" out of the way, I was off to the races.

In order to check my constraint by computer search command, I defined a word as how it is spelled. I allowed plurals and tense changes, hyphenated combinations, portmanteaus, contractions, and some words from other languages, assuming that the less I resorted to these variants, the better the novel would be. I also decided to rely more on my regular vocabulary than on words whose meanings I would forget once I dug them out of the dictionary, & for some reason that smacks of learning to ride a bike with training wheels, I allowed an unlimited use of the ampersand.

At first, I was mostly interested in practicing how to write sentences and paragraphs that made sense without little words. After fifty pages, my computer crashed.

In the weeks it took to find out that all was lost, I kept practicing in longhand. Soon a plot sprang from the opening sentence, of a gambler who resolves to reform himself by doing what he has not done before. He would go from job to job and town to town, in search of new nouns, verbs, adjectives. Fairly early in the composition process, I saw the complete narrative arc. My essential problem spun off of Einstein's infinite-but-bound model of the universe, where the gravitational forces from heavenly bodies bend beams of light to lead a person with an infinite gaze to stare at the back of her head. The "write what you know" maxim of the creative writing class played off a central objective of writing via constraints: by forcing yourself to write in ways you normally wouldn't use, you could write what you didn't think you knew. As infinite as the possibilities may seem, we're limited by what we know and discover, so as much as my character might try to get away from what he had done before, he was doomed to return to where he began.

Newspaper crime reports, scenes in books and movies, and snatches of conversations informed vignettes and situations, but the real work for me was to go from word to word, and later to look for repeated words by using the F keys on a Word for Dos 6 program. I wrote one or two sentences a day, sometimes half of a page, in sessions of one to three hours. At the same period, I was trying to write an unconstrained novel, and the compositional crawl of *Never Again* made it easy to write fluid, conventional prose. I soon lost interest in whatever that other project was.

I showed a few people an early version, dumped the ampersands, revised to make it more comprehensible, and put it aside. Time is a formidable editor, and manuscripts built from untried constraints need much more time in the drawer between revisions than other manuscripts need.

Some years later, about a decade after I began writing the book, I read *Never Again* again. It seemed likely that I wouldn't understand what was happening; or, worse, that I'd fall into the trap of the overconfident horseplayer, who blithely picks winners out of old stacks of the *Daily Racing Form* from past performances of foregone conclusions, as if unaware of results that are destined to be unforgettable. I was afraid that no matter how tangled the prose was, I couldn't help but understand what was going on.

At this point, I wasn't proofreading, and even though some passages annoyed me and would have to be redone, I wasn't looking to revise. I only wanted to read the book as if I had just picked it off a shelf.

A few chapters in, there's a scene in which many desperate unemployed laborers line up to apply for a single job in a steel mill. One of the many, who had nearly burned to death in an accident at that mill, isn't out for work but for revenge. Somewhere between the description setting the scene and the moment the man opens fire, an authorial aside comments on NAFTA, capitalism, and the inevitable exporting of jobs to Mexico. I thought, what is this—Dickens? And then I realized what it was, and that even if it wasn't yet done, I knew it was going to get there.

The Cross as Lynching Tree in Leon Forrest's There is a Tree More Ancient than Eden

DANA A. WILLIAMS

I remember the first time I read Leon Forrest's *There Is a Tree More Ancient than Eden.* I had never encountered anything like it—so rich, so complex, so lyrical, so enlightening, so mysterious, all at once. Notably, I wasn't alone in feeling whelmed after reading (and re-reading) the novel's final pages. In the Foreword of this deceptively thin novel of 214 pages, Ralph Ellison writes:

> As I began to get my bearings in the reeling world of *There Is a Tree More Ancient than Eden*, I thought, *What a tortured, history-wracked, anguished, Hound-of-Heaven-pursued, Ham-and-Oedipus-cursed, Blake-visioned, apolcalypse-prone projection of the human predicament! . . . How admirable the manner in which the great themes of life and literature are revealed in the black-white, white-black American-ness of his characters as dramatized in the cathedral-high and cloaca-low limits of his imaginative ranging.*
>
> So, I read on, bouncing between moods of tragic contemplation and bursts of hilarious laughter, between speculations upon the shifting relationships between the American myth of democracy and everyday reality, brooding over his evocations of those

> dilemmas bred of Christian faith and racial conflict, of
> social violence, family friction and dreams of a
> peaceful kingdom . . .

Ellison's cataloguing of even these few of the many discourses the novel engages, from biblical and mythical texts to American democracy's fraught ideals, indeed begins to capture Forrest's "imaginative ranging", a range made possible in large part by the diversity of his background. Leon Forrest was as comfortable with street hustlers and blues that found themselves in bars (where he worked for years while writing) as he was straddling the liminal space between the ritualism of Catholicism and the secular traditions that found their ways into the improvisational traditions of Protestantism. Undeniably, a person too unfamiliar with the many deep layers of black culture could never survive in this "reeling world."

The novel opens with its main character Nathaniel (Turner) Witherspoon, who is more like the person through whose eyes the novel is focalized than he is a traditional character, in crisis and struggling to make sense of his mother's death. Even as his situation is highly personal and particularized, in some ways, Nathaniel becomes the embodiment of an *everyman*, as he accesses memories of more general black experiences through his memories about and recollections of other characters who populate 'The Lives' section of the novel. In that section, we encounter family members, folk characters, and historical figures like Harriet Tubman, Frederick Douglass, Louis Armstrong, and Abraham Lincoln. Each character has left some imprint on Nathaniel's memory of his mother and of his understanding of contemporary black life. The sections that follow, 'The Nightmare' and 'The Dream', build on the theme of the motherlessness as Nathaniel grapples with the trauma of the Middle Passage and the Underground Railroad. The memories he sorts through of these experiences lead him to a dream about the most fruitful responses to nightmare. Should he assume the ideology of Jericho Witherspoon, the formerly enslaved jurist who lives to be 117 and who believes that suffering is universal and that it facilitates creativity? Or should he adopt the position of Jamestown Fishbond, whose identifying mark is his "unusual, deep, abiding blackness" and who is a trickster savant known to have countless aliases, many of whom are of white men—including confederates Jefferson Davis and Nathan Forrest. Unlike Jericho, Jamestown recognizes the unique horror in African American suffering and believes that Nathaniel must learn to transform the suffering before he can ever learn to celebrate an inevitable victory over it. All of this leads to what seems to me to be the centerpiece of the novel, the section entitled 'The Vision'.

Struggling to determine which aspects of history he should retain and which he should discard, Nathaniel must deal with the "evocations of those dilemmas bred of Christian faith and racial conflict, of social violence, family friction and dreams of a peaceful kingdom" Ellison alludes to in his Foreword. And like Nathaniel, the reader must make sense of the evocations as well. In that sense, understanding 'The Vision' is at least one key to understanding the novel. The problem with this, however, is that it takes a bit more than traditional approaches to literature to "understand" 'The Vision'. Literary scholars tend to read the novel in the tradition of James Joyce's *Ulysses* and other quest narratives. And in some ways, Nathaniel's journey can be likened to a quest. But traditional readings of him as a "hero" (in the Kenneth Burke tradition) leave so much wanting. Part of the novel's goal is to disrupt master narratives, so using those tools to attempt to read *There Is a Tree More Ancient than Eden* falls flat rather than enlivens the novel. Again, Ellison's insight provides us with a lighted path. The dilemmas bred of the intersections of Christianity, racial conflict, and violence must be unpacked and resolved. In walks James Cones's *The Cross and the Lynching Tree*.

For thirty pages of the novel, the cross and the lynching tree become one. And while Forrest isn't the only author who wrestles with the racial violence that informs the cross—Richard Wright has Bigger Thomas excoriate the crucifix that represents his mother's religion because he recognizes it as the proverbial lynching tree of his execution; and Bigger's recognition is but one popular of many—*There Is a Tree More Ancient than Eden* probably sustains the critique of these intersections longer and does so more explicitly than any other literary text. As Cone notes, literary authors have long been more willing than ministers to explore the relation of the cross and the lynching tree. Forrest is no exception in this regard, and few have done it better.

As the opening scene of 'The Vision' unfolds, the man to be lynched/crucified is pierced in his side (though unlike Jesus, he *does* utter a mumbling word), and someone "rebel yells" three times—*he is a nigger*. Time collapses as the biblical past merges with the contemporary highly racialized moment: there are bloodhounds, the crowd queries if they shall castrate him; and dismemberment ensues. The man's body parts are cut and flung about, but the crowd is not satisfied until he is decapitated, and his head is placed in the river. The imagery throughout reminds us that this particular lynching tree is "more ancient than Eden", so the classical African creation myth is invoked too. The two leaders preparing the scene are locked together sphinx like, thus alluding to Egypt. And even after the man is dismembered, the crowd is still dissatisfied; perhaps remembering Osiris's return after Isis (re)members him, they want his soul.

As the event progresses, "a band of bruised-blood angels" wearing chains on their ankles (evoking slavery imagery) and bloodied rosaries, begin to gather the man's rotted parts. A ritual (with the bloodied rosaries as our first clue that rituals can easily go terribly wrong) on the banks of the river begins with an old-fashioned baptismal, a three-year-old child (who is put in the angels' sackcloth), and women and men singing and clapping their hands. The sackcloth the angels have placed the baby and the man's parts in begins to get heavier and larger. Eventually it explodes, and the man's form rises up totally collected in its original form with the man holding the baby in his arms. His wings are broken, like limb branches torn from their plantation roots; his mouth is twisted, and his head bloody, but "Lord father he was flying flying flying."

Interestingly, I have always read 'The Vision' as the key section of

There Is a Tree More Ancient than Eden. But now more than ever, in the time of hashtags like #blacklivesmatter, we would do well to consider carefully the implications of the tension between sustained reflection and swift thought—and 'The Vision' calls us to do just that. One heightens the discourses; the other promotes commentary but with little to no attending movement toward any real achievement that can be called liberating. What Cone's *The Cross and the Lynching Tree* does, as the latest book in his articulation of liberation theology, is help us to see that Forrest's *There Is a Tree More Ancient than Eden* calls us to affirm that the black experience as a grounding moment is a legitimate lens through which to view and to understand critical elements of theology—creation, death, and resurrection. Both Cone and Forrest argue convincingly that contextual theologies are as legitimate as theologies that take the revelation of God as a point of departure. One isn't more legitimate than the other, but one is viewed in academic circles as more divinely begotten and therefore more right. The failure of literary studies to point us in this direction is mitigated by the openness of liberation theology, which, ironically, struggled mightily to gain credence in religious studies.

The hard work theology does at its best is to reveal to us how people respond in moments of existential and epistemological crisis so we might imagine how best to ground ourselves after the center collapses. *There Is a Tree More Ancient than Eden* and *The Cross and the Lynching Tree* extend and do this work, first and foremost by imploring us to believe in the primacy of a black experience. To understand how and why black lives in particular matter, it is critical to understand that no other point of entry (even as all lives matter indeed) provides the cultural grounding necessary to grapple hermeneutically or epistemologically with our understandings of humanity in its fullness. In other words, the texts seem to tell us, it would be foolish to yield the point that one cannot begin from the point of her own experience as a legitimate understanding of human and divine existence and about the discourses that attend matters of divinity and spirit, especially when survival is at stake.

This perhaps why for many years the black writer saw the preacher as the bard of the race. Toni Morrison recognizes it not just in Baby Suggs in *Beloved* but also in the essay 'The Site of Memory', where she argues that what makes her literature distinctly black is its effort to replicate a black church experience where the individual is safe in, distinct from, and a part of (all at the same time) the community. All of these intersections of religion and racial conflict and violence consistently beckon us to embrace and then to nurture sustained theological reflection. And 'The Vision' section makes clear the futility of the practical/theoretical divide. In reality or lived experience, the novel reminds us, there is no chasm to breach. The contemplative moment, the moment of vision, is our most viable path to "Wakefulness" and "Transformation."

*Reveries of Desire: An Interview with Rikki Ducornet**

STEVEN MOORE

Rikki Ducornet has led a life almost as exotic as that of any of her characters. Born in 1943 in New York, she traveled extensively as a child, was a beatnik in high school, then attended Bard College to take a degree in art. In the 1960s she began exhibiting her work with fellow surrealists, and since then has exhibited throughout the world. After marrying, she moved with her husband to Algeria, then to Canada, and finally to France, where they lived in a small village in the Loire Valley for many years. Though she had already written and illustrated a few children's books, it wasn't until the 1970s that she began writing in earnest: first poems and short tales (the latter were gathered into a book called *The Butcher's Tales* and published in Canada in a limited edition in 1980), and then her first novel, *The Stain*, a tale of demonic possession set in a French village like the one she lived in at the time. It was published by Chatto & Windus in England in 1984 (and by Grove Press here) and became the first in a tetralogy: *Entering Fire* followed in 1986, and *The Fountains of Neptune* in 1989, by which time Ducornet had returned to the U.S. (without her husband) and accepted a position teaching at the University of Denver, where she is novelist in residence.

The Fountains of Neptune had been published only in Canada; she sent a copy of it along with a chapter from her next novel to Dalkey Archive

---

* First published in *The Bloomsbury Review*, January/February 1998, p. 11-12, republished with permission.

Press for possible U.S. distribution. I was an editor there at the time and fell in love with her work. Thereafter, Dalkey Archive published one Ducornet book a year: the U.S. edition of *The Fountains of Neptune* in 1992, *The Jade Cabinet* in 1993—which concluded her tetralogy and was a finalist for the National Book Critics Circle award for fiction—an expanded edition of *The Complete Butcher's Tales* in 1994, and a revised version of *The Stain* and her latest novel, *Phosphor in Dreamland*, in 1995. She received many awards, most notably a Lannan Literary Fellowship for Fiction.

A new collection of stories, *The Word "Desire"*, was published by Holt in October 1997, by which time Ducornet was already at work on two more books: a novel about the Marquis de Sade (and the Inquisition's activities in the New World) entitled *The Fan-maker's Inquistion*, and a fanciful encyclopedia based on one of Jorge Luis Borges' enigmatic tales. The following interview took place at her home just as *The Word "Desire"* was arriving in bookstores.

*

Steven Moore (SM): I've always thought of you as a kind of literary belly dancer: your work is very sensuous and exotic (and sometimes even set in the Middle East). You're working in a venerable tradition that nevertheless is looked down upon by puritans, you're practicing an art that is rigorous and abandoned, and so forth. Are you offended by the comparison?

Rikki Ducornet (RD): It's a curious one; I'm surprised [laughing], taken aback! But who isn't intrigued by belly dancers? The first time I saw one I was a little child, so maybe there's something to that. She was wonderful, my first . . .

SM: Role model as an artist?

RD: Maybe she was! I was not quite 11 years old when my father had received a Fulbright in Egypt. All the Fulbright people were taken one night to a tent some place in the desert, not far from the pyramids, and this gorgeous redhead showed up, I'd never seen a belly dancer; I had no idea they existed, but I was just getting interested in the sensuous world, and I was fascinated. She had bells at her ankles and wrists, and she was very self-possessed!

SM: What a great female role model to initiate you into the world of art. I used the terms "sensuous" and "exotic"; those are two words used to describe Anais Nin's writings. Do you feel any connection with writings of her generation, like Marguerite Young, other pioneers?

RD: I've not read Marguerite Young yet, though I'm about to this winter. But Anais Nin I read voraciously as a young woman. In fact I had some wonderful first editions—I wonder where they are now?—*Cities of the Interior, A Spy in the House of Love,* when I was 15 or 16 I was also reading Isak Dinesen and Henry Miller and the existential writers: Camus and Sartre, Kierkegaard. However, Kafka was the writer I loved best, and later on Borges, who had himself been profoundly influenced by Kafka.

SM: Were you doing any writing at that time?

RD: Mostly in the form of love letters [laughs], while smoking Camels. I'm glad I survived!

SM: You dressed all in black, I imagine, that sort of thing?

RD: I was the only beatnik in Red Hook Central High School. I was also reading Jack Kerouac, Ferlinghetti, Ginsberg, and I think they kept me sane.

SM: It must have been a great thrill to be published by Ferlinghetti's City Lights years later.

RD: It was wonderful, tremendously exciting. Actually the boyfriend I was writing these love letters to was constantly leaving school to go west since he'd read *On the Road.* I think there were maybe three of us at the school who had read *On the Road* . . . and *The Subterraneans,* that was a great one. I tried very hard to look like Mardou Fox!

SM: All these writers you've mentioned write in the present, yet most of your work is set in the past. What is it about writing historical fiction that interests you?

RD: Egypt obviously had a profound impression on my imagination as a child. I loved Egypt, as did my father. We did a lot of walking in Cairo and explored Luxor, Carnak, the Valley of the Kings, and so on. I felt aesthetically at home; I loved the things I saw—the sculpture, temples, and paintings—and was fascinated by the hieroglyphs, studied them, and copied them into my drawing book. The very distant past resonated in a very special way. I recall how the light strikes the great temple in Carnak; most of the roof is gone and the columns block the sun, create mysterious shadows. The walls are carved with the wonderful figures of Horus, Anubis, Isis, and all the anthropomorphic gods come alive as the sun moves across the sky. I still dream about Egypt, actually.

SM: Some of the most memorable sections of *The Jade Cabinet* are set in Egypt.

RD: The perfect setting for a mad architect and a thwarted lover! Later I lived in Algeria for two years and visited the Roman ruins there. But also as a young girl, I read a vast amount of French literature—Flaubert, Stendhal, Proust—and became very much a Francophile, so that's part of it too.

SM: And you seem to have an affection for some of the more eccentric aspects of Victorian culture, especially "nonsense" writers like Lewis Carroll and Edward Lear.

RD: I think nonsense is tremendously serious, though it's not didactic, It usually involves social commentary of some kind, often very vicious!

SM: So it's the nonsense writers, rather than the more staid ones like George Eliot, that interest you?

RD: I liked them too, and my early readings of the Victorians certainly helped in the writing of *The Jade Cabinet*, but it's true that the ones who had the greatest impact on my imagination were Lear and Lewis Carroll. As did Jonathan Swift, who now comes to mind. And I was reading Sade as a young girl; my father was very trusting that way, and gave me *Justine* when I was about 17.

SM: You said that nonsense writers are often social critics. Do your historical fictions function as parables, as commentaries on our own times?

RD: Very much so. One of the primary reasons I've been so stubborn about writing about the 19th century is that I see it as a period of transition when industry and capital really took over. All the seeds of what we see now in terms of political and ecological devastation were being sown then.

SM: Especially in *Entering Fire*, though that's set a little closer to our time.

RD: I was very conscious of writing about the end of Eden, the forces—political, religious, and economic—that led to the Holocaust. I was researching the roots of anti-Semitism in France, how French fascism came about, why the French were so eager to embrace the Nazis. The French terror of the Jew goes back to the Middle Ages and comes to a head in the 20th century. There's a paradox I wished to investigate. On the one hand, the 19th century was a time when infinite progress was thought possible, there was an intense yearning towards the future, and so on; but simultaneously alienation, oppression, and unlimited industrialization were growing apace.

SM: The books suggest a great depth of research.

RD: Writing is a wonderful excuse to indulge one's curiosity. But also I want to have books historically rooted: even if I fracture history, even if I do perverse things with it, I know what I'm fracturing, and what is being perverted. Often a book goes in very unexpected directions because of the research. I'm working on a new book about the Marquis de Sade and the French Revolution's "Terror" as a mirror of violence in the New World. During the research into the Inquisition in the Yucatan, I realized Sade's obsessions were also the Inquisitor Bishop Landa's and the Church's obsessions, especially sodomy, which was one of the primary justifications for the destruction of the Indian populations, who were said to be sodomites.

SM: Was Sade aware of Bishop Landa, or is that your connection?

RD: It's my connection. I wanted to put two monsters together: Bishop Landa, who was responsible for the deaths of thousands and the destruction of eight centuries of Mayan culture, and Sade, who wrote about sexual murder but never murdered anyone, yet is perceived as a monster. That is the curious paradox at the heart of the book.

SM: Despite your love for historical settings, do you think you'll ever write a book with a contemporary setting?

RD: All of these books touch on power, the abuse of authority, and the craziness of orthodoxies. In *Entering Fire*, I very briefly touched on the McCarthy era, so yes, I think the next time around I'd like to write a book finally that would take place in the United States, and maybe for a change be very autobiographical.

SM: You were a young girl at that time.

RD: I remember watching the McCarthy hearings on television, and putting together a puppet show with little friends. I made a McCarthy puppet with bristles and a nasal "quack".

SM: The eccentric scholar is a recurring type in your books: Angus Sphery in *The Jade Cabinet*, several protagonists in *The Word "Desire"*, even the narrator of your current "encyclopedia of Tlön" project. What attracts you to this type?

RD: I think all of these characters are based on my father. My father was an eccentric scholar—which is why there were all those books in the house—an eccentric man who always, throughout my infancy, was involved with war games. He had created an imaginary world with little trees, oceans, and cities, and by the time he died he could fight any battle in the history of mankind, including with Neanderthals. But I have memories of grown men showing up and fighting the Battle of Waterloo. He was also involved in an international game: his own country was called the Kingdom of Elir—in French, Le Royaume d'Elir—the kingdom of the elect. But if you think about it, d'Elir also means "delirium" [French *délire*], which I don't think he ever considered.

SM: The Kingdom of the Mad!

RD: The Kingdom of the Delirious! Actually, Robert Coover, when he was writing *The Universal Baseball Association*, met my father. He was amused at the war games and spent some time watching them and taking notes. Men with dice! When you have a really eccentric father as a child, it leaves a strong impression. He was fascinating and delightful in may ways, but somehow kind of mad, a lot like Angus Sphery.

SM: You've talked about the influence Egypt had on you, but you also lived many years in France. Aside from providing the setting for your first novel, how did France influence you?

RD: It was compelling and startling to live in a place "left behind" in the past. There was a Merovingian graveyard in the village, buildings that dated from the Renaissance, and a superstitious people. The Catholic Church had a real hold on the village, which was really run by nuns, who were all right-wingers. In addition to the harm they did generally, they would get the villagers to vote for people like Le Pen.

SM: Did you get along with those villagers?

RD: I did. I didn't get along with the nuns, and I had some sporadic difficulty with the neighbors because a number of them were alcoholics. These were very impoverished people, I was living among agricultural workers. But I got along with some of them very well. My son grew up in that village, so I knew the children intimately and watched them grow up. But at times it was a battle against superstition. The neighbors, for example, wouldn't go to the doctor when they were hurt; if a child was burned they would go to the *"rabouteu"*, which was a witch doctor, and have the fire "conjured" away. That was astonishing! Medieval! And dangerous! And there was a woman who had lived in the house behind me who everyone said was a witch; they were convinced she had bewitched them, all at one time or another. She believed it herself.

SM: So even though *The Stain* is set in the 1880s, the events almost could have occurred in the 1970s when you lived there.

RD: Yes. And that's what really started my interest in research too, because I realized when I began to write the novel that I wanted to write about that place, that I wanted to write about the 19th century, because so much of what I'd seen and heard seemed to evoke a not-too-distant past. I did an enormous amount of research for that book and to my enchantment, discovered that the way people spoke, the way they ate, the little fête that would take place down in my part of the village with pancakes and accordion music, the marriages—all these things were exactly as they had been in the 19th century. The only difference would be, for example, that during the wedding ceremony somebody would bring out a little plastic record player; that was the only modern thing, except that maybe the way people were dressed, but otherwise the traditional games and jokes were being played. The game of the garter I described in *The Stain* I saw: the bride having to move the garter up and down depending on how much people were bidding. I fell in love with that village, because walking into the village was always like walking into a dream of the past. The landscape is unchanged even now, and even the little grocery store, with its silk thread and brown soap and old ladies gossiping . . .

SM: Why did you finally leave?

RD: It had been a wonderful experience to be there as a writer, alone with English, playing English against French—it is a fascinating dilemma for a writer: to grapple with two languages. But I was beginning to feel isolated intellectually: I wasn't living in Paris, I was living in a small, impoverished village in the Val de Loire, among vineyard workers, mushroom growers, and extremely right-wing people. It was very lonely. I applied to the Bunting Institute at Radcliffe in order to be with creative people—above all creative women. I knew some extraordinarily creative people in France, for the most part street-theater people. But they were often away, and I was beginning to miss writers. I also felt I needed to get back to English, that I could lose touch.

SM: How did *The Word "Desire"* come about? I remember about two years ago, you began sending me an occasional story. Did you envision a cohesive collection back then?

RD: I was craving to write a somewhat "classic" book of short stories, "classic" in terms of structure but also in terms of size, because most of the stories in the previous story book, *The Butcher's Tales*, were often miniscule. And I knew from the start I wanted to explore the theme of desire.

SM: The stories cover almost every form of desire, from sexual desire to various thwarted, even twisted forms.

RD: *The Word "Desire"* is not only about sexual longing and famishment, it is about how hard it is to be human; it is about childhood and repression—

political, sexual, psychological. In an oasis in the Algerian Sahara, I once saw a beautiful women reveal—in a flash of fire—her hennaed hands and feet to a stranger. That image is the invisible cipher or potency burning at the heart of the book.

SM: The collection is not called simply *Desire* but *The Word "Desire"*, with the emphasis on desire as a literary construct, as a force that not only moves people but creates literary form.

RD: I see the title story as a kind of philosophical reverie about what it is to be human. The woman narrator recognizes the lover's intrinsic right to acknowledge the erotic potency of another, that this capacity is born of a generous and loving impulse, that this is the nature of what it is to be profoundly alive. We are creatures of fire—this is what she comes to see. The book is really about being creatures of reverie, on way or another. Of course reveries can turn into nightmares.

SM: In addition to the novel about Sade, you're working on something having to do with Borges's imaginary region called Tlön. Can you tell us about that?

RD: Years ago I illustrated Borges's *Tlön, Uqbar, Orbis Tertius* [published by The Porcupine's Quill, 1983], and while I was doing that, I thought it would be wonderful someday to do an encyclopedia of Tlön, from A to Z, Alpha to Zodiac. So I've begun it, with encyclopedic entries, which I'll be illustrating, with references to games, sexuality, myths, gems. Borges was enamored of Lewis Carroll and Kafka, so I'm also reading the writers— Herodotus is another—who were tremendously important for Borges. In this way I hope to write something in the Borgesian spirit somehow. I don't want to write a parody!

SM: Let's end with a trivial question: I understand that you are the referent in Steely Dan's song "Rikki Don't Lose That Number". How did that come about?

RD: I knew Donald Fagen at Bard. He was wildly gifted. He gave me a phone number which I never used and I guess I lost! Philosophically it's an interesting song; I mean I think his "number" is a cipher for the self.

SM: Well, you're immortalized in pop culture now.

Gilbert Adair Continued

JAMES LANGDON

THE MONSTROSITY OF INFLUENCE

I remember a television documentary that Channel 4 produced about Donald Judd after he died. I watched it in a video library in the basement of the monolithic concrete art block at Coventry University. Matthew Collings presented, looking very English, standing in the scorching Texan desert outside Judd's compound. A talking head contemporary of Judd's, Richard Serra, explained how Don began his career as an art critic and used his monotone reviews of painting exhibitions to foreshadow his own elementary sculptures. I can't actually recall, but I assume Collings delivered a comic parody of Judd's writing. Something like: "There is a painting. It is red. There is another painting. It is green. A yellow band extends from its bottom left corner half way along its bottom edge . . ." and so on. What I took from Serra's commentary was the idea that Judd's bluntly styled prose was a kind of hoax, preempting his appearance as an artist, setting the scene for artworks best described by their technical specifications. Serra, having introduced this notion, proclaimed it to be "very clever", in an admiring, slightly resentful way.

Another preemptive art-hoax is plotted in Scottish author Gilbert Adair's 1998 novel, *A Key of the Tower*. Sacha Liebermann is an academic, a leading authority on the work of the 17th-century painter Georges de La Tour, and he authors the definitive monograph on the artist. This apparently scholarly publication is in fact an elaborate deception whose entire, carefully disguised purpose is to canonize a La Tour painting that, so Liebermann reports, has been missing since 1885, and presumably destroyed. Secretly, in his studio, he has been forging — inventing — this work that in fact never existed. He and his accomplice, Beatrice, the wife of an unsuspecting art dealer, plan to "discover" the fictional painting, sell it to an unscrupulous collector for ten million pounds and elope. The hoax is foiled in the novel's conclusion, and Liebermann murderously undone.

Both narratives subversively anticipate artworks. Judging by Liebermann's fate in *A Key of the Tower*, Adair thought this contrivance distasteful. So consider the following inversion of the motif. There exists an obscure breed of writer known as the "anticipatory plagiarist." This term was apparently invented at the Ouvroir de littérature potentielle (workshop for potential literature) to describe Charles Lutwidge Dodgson, the English author who, under the pen name Lewis Carroll, wrote *Alice's Adventures in Wonderland*. The Oulipo, a collective of writers and mathematicians founded in Paris in 1960, saw in Carroll an artist who had already formulated, a century before, the union of literary imagination and procedural writing devices that they aspired to. The label was a disarmingly mischievous acknowledgement of the derivative nature of THEIR project.

To be derivative is stigmatic, especially in literature. Gilbert Adair was the most exemplary of derivative writers, but, in the same mischievous spirit of the Oulipo, his relations with the canon were promiscuous and unfettered. His was a consistent artistic proposition: practically everything he wrote was a continuation of the work of another writer. He wrote novels, criticism and commentary (often on the subject of cinema), biography, translation, and adaptations for the screen. He wrote continuations of Carroll's *Alice* and J. M. Barrie's *Peter Pan*, recreating and extending their fictions and prose with extraordinary technical fidelity. He pastiched Agatha Christie in a trilogy of murder mysteries. He made a cultural translation of Roland Barthes' *Mythologies* (meaning he translated not the text, but the project, substituting Barthes' survey of French cultural references with English equivalents). He wrote a biography of the real life boy who inspired Thomas Mann's novella *Death in Venice*, and a novel, *Love and Death on Long Island*, whose portrait of obsession is an homage to Mann's book.

Continuity even pervades Adair's imagery. Returning to *A Key of the Tower*, the opening scene has two men—one of them the previously mentioned unsuspecting art dealer, the other a lonely writer—driving in opposite directions along a remote road in the French countryside. It is night, and there is a wild storm. Lightning strikes the moment before they will pass, bringing down a tree and blocking the road between their two vehicles. At the roadside, the two strangers consider their predicament. Eventually, they resolve that the only way for them to continue their journeys is to swap cars. The exchange proceeds clumsily as the writer, having handed over the keys to his dilapidated Mini, struggles to master the controls of the art dealer's pristine Rolls-Royce.

Adair himself was consummately skilled in mastering the mechanisms of other writers. He achieved literary notoriety for his translation of Georges Perec's *La Disparition* from French into English, a project that occupied him for four years. Perec was the iconic member of the Oulipo, and his extraordinary novel is a lipogram on the letter "e", meaning that letter—the most commonly occurring in both French and English—does not appear once in its 300+ pages. Adair's version, titled *A Void*, is not only a translation of the original's narrative, but of its technical virtuosity. By translating a lipogram into a lipogram, Adair was outdoing the already impossibly prohibitive constraint of the original. I could go on, but the point is this: from entire fictions to a single letter, Adair worked in explicit relation to the writers he admired. He found a name for this practice via another French literary academic, Gérard Genette, who termed it "transtextual."

A FINISHED WORK REQUIRES URGENT RESUSCITATION

In September 2010, I initiated an interview with Adair. I wanted to understand his perspective on the canon, to situate him on a continuum between what I perceived as the two polar philosophies that his work might represent. At one pole, I imagined Adair a postmodern nihilist, scoffing at originality and engaged in a kind of morbid, joyless exercise in imitation. At the other pole, a more pragmatic position, in which the technical and aesthetic elements of a literary style are not bound to the identity of their author, but, once published, become vehicles for other writers to use in unforeseen ways. I got an email address from his agent and contacted Adair to propose the interview. I said that I would try to get the result published. He responded and agreed to a conversation over email.

James: *Alice Through the Needle's Eye* is written as a continuation of Lewis Carroll's two classics, *Alice's Adventures in Wonderland* and *Through the Looking Glass*. Like Carroll's originals, your text employs circular narratives and imagery. Your method seems to have something in common with the monographs of Gilles Deleuze, who described his portraits of philosophical predecessors Nietzsche, Kant, Spinoza and Bergson as forms of buggery: "I saw myself as taking an author from behind and giving him a child that would be his own offspring, yet monstrous." Much of your subsequent fiction is informed by this idea of continuity. You refer to repetitions, continuing the journeys of others and so on. You have accounted for the history and status of this genre in your essay 'On Transtextuality', but how did you proceed practically? What were the mechanics of appropriating Lewis Carroll's voice, for example? How did you begin?

Gilbert: I had never come across the Deleuze quote, but actually find it extremely interesting and pertinent, even if anatomically more than suspect (no one has ever had a child, however monstrous, by being taken

> from behind). I just hope it's not too urgent, as I'm a
> bit swamped with work at the moment and the
> question is not really one to which I can dash off an
> answer in ten minutes or so. Is there a deadline? Or are
> you able to wait until I have some proper breathing
> space?

I replied to say that there was no deadline, and—pleased that my reference appeared to have got his attention—that it would not be a problem for the response to be delayed. But nothing followed. I wrote a further polite reminder. No response. The interview had stalled. Until, a year later, I read Gilbert's obituary. I learned that in 2010, he had suffered a debilitating stroke, leaving him almost blind. A distinguished author blinded, unable to read or write without assistance: I recognized immediately the tragic parallel to the plot of Gilbert's own novel, *A Closed Book*. Following this grave news, I reread 'On Transtextuality.' There, Gilbert casually outlines a project for a prospective apprentice to take up: "Consider Cocteau's celebrated monodrama, *The Human Voice*, whose middle-aged heroine makes one last, despairing telephone call to the lover who is on the point of abandoning her. It is possible to imagine a reworking of that play that would focus instead on the other end of the telephone connection, on the abandoning lover. Nor would it strain a competent writer's powers of invention to devise some new, transtextual title (*The Inhuman Voice?*). Then that writer has to get down to the workaday chore of writing the thing, from line to line, from page to page, and the problems he confronts are liable to be just as formidable as those necessitated by a completely original scenario. The more so as he will naturally seek to avoid treading on the Master's toes."

It occurred to me that I might take *The Inhuman Voice* as an invitation to resuscitate my interview with Gilbert. First, I would need a method for simulating his voice. Anyone superficially familiar with Gilbert's fiction probably would have arrived first at the same obvious approach: to compose his responses to my questions by excerpting from his texts.

Surely an insightful meta-narrative would be revealed that way. I assembled some promising passages and made a start:

> James: Let me begin with the same question as before. You have accounted for the history and status of the transtextual, but how did you proceed practically? What were the mechanics of appropriating Lewis Carroll's voice, for example? How did you begin?
>
> Found-Gilbert: Were one to see a man with a horse's head, one would not cry, "Look! A man with a horse's head!", but "Look! A centaur!" And were one to see a woman with a fish's tail, one would not cry "Look! A woman with a fish's tail!" but "Look! A mermaid!" A centaur is a centaur, a mermaid is a mermaid. Mythological (in the word's more orthodox usage) as they are, such creatures have come to possess in our eyes (or in our imagination) their own compact and specific identities: if they are "singular", then it is in the sense both of uniqueness and oneness.

Was that Gilbert's head on Carroll's body, or the other way around? I looked for further clues in the texts and uncovered nothing. In any case, Found-Gilbert's enigmatic response had pointed out the flimsy premise in my approach. I had ignored an important distinction: Gilbert's writing is always more reconstituted than found, more *monstrous*.

Simulating Gilbert would require a more subtle appraisal of his work. In other essays I noted Gilbert rehearsing positions that he might have taken had our conversation continued. In 'Black and White in Colour' he criticizes the practice of retrospectively colorizing black and white films: "Since black and white cinematography is coterminous with a fairly precise era of film history, colorization represents an anachronism as indefensible as would be the engrafting of a belated soundtrack onto a silent classic." 'On Updating' is an equally severe dismissal of the early

2000s trend for productions of stage classics in contemporary scenarios—Shakespeare with mobile phones and the like. "No one has ever reorchestrated a Bruckner symphony in the hope of appealing to fans of Sondheim or Take That. No one has ever repainted a Rembrandt self-portrait on the grounds that the sight of a wrinkled old codger in a 17th-century smock would prove alienating to a spectator of the nineties." This last excerpt may contain the essence of Gilbert's sensibility. The friction contained in a sentence comparing Take That AND Bruckner was what seemed to delight him. Not Bruckner BY Take That, just simply Bruckner AND Take That AND . . .

This was an instructive realization. A recreation of Gilbert's voice must express something previously unsaid, however derivative. Accordingly, I devised an alternative format for the interview. I would write to friends and colleagues of Gilbert, asking them to respond to one of my original questions, as if in Gilbert's voice. I initially sent two emails, one to a noted Oulipian whose address I obtained through the Parisian gallery where he exhibits sculptures. No responses. Discouraged, I revisited Cocteau and *The Human Voice*. Perhaps I ought to take the speculative outline of *The Inhuman Voice* even more literally.

THE INHUMAN VOICE

CereProc is a digital voice synthesis production studio based at Edinburgh University. I discovered their work through an online video of a TED talk titled 'Remaking my Voice', given by journalist and screenwriter Roger Ebert in 2011. Ebert had lost his speech while suffering from throat cancer. In the video, he demonstrates various voice synthesis systems and has family and colleagues speak for him, reading from scripts. He describes how his dissatisfaction with generic computerized voices led him to seek a more personal tool to express himself, and ultimately to the production of a unique simulation of his voice, made by CereProc, using archive recordings provided by Ebert himself.

Intrigued by the prospect of a posthumous digital synthesis of Gilbert's voice, I searched for suitable material. Gilbert's friend David Thompson kindly agreed to send me a copy of a compilation of clips of Gilbert on television and film that he had prepared for a memorial. Gilbert made cameos in film adaptations of his novels and appeared regularly as a critic and presenter on the BBC's *The Late Show*. In the first clip on the DVD, he is seen talking about Jean Cocteau again, standing in front of a Cocteau fresco, praising the various output of the French visual artist, writer, filmmaker, and boxing trainer. Expecting to hear a Scottish accent, I was surprised that Gilbert's delivery has a measured, southern English character to it. (I later learned that his speaking style is a good example of Received Pronunciation, the archetypal form of broadcast English.) He slips effortlessly between English and French as he recites titles and quotations from Cocteau. How fitting that his voice should conform to a conventional idea of neutrality. Nonetheless, Gilbert's diction did have some distinctive characteristics. He seemed to relish constructing certain words in his mouth, such as "evol-yew-shun" and "otto-matic."

I made contact with the executors of Gilbert's estate, again solicited by his agent. They responded to say that they did indeed have some audio, and asked for what purposes I intended to use it. I wrote enthusiastically, explaining that I was researching the possibility of making a synthesis of Gilbert's voice so that I could finish a conversation that I had started with him. This may have been poorly judged.

I also found references online to recorded lectures by Gilbert. An inquiry with one academic institution prompted an unsettling episode. On the morning of 22 October 2013, two years after his death, I received an email from Gilbert Adair. Subject: "My voice." It reads: "I got a message from Surrey University saying you wanted to get a recording from them because you're making a computer synthesized version of my voice. I'll probably be happy to give permission for this, but I am intrigued . . . could you fill me in a bit more on the project?" There is another Gilbert Adair, a poet. I suppressed my embarrassment and considered whether this was opportune. Should I ask this Living-Gilbert to answer my questions? Too farcical. Then should I ask Living-Gilbert to impersonate Dead-Gilbert for a recording? Have him try to learn and reproduce the character of Dead-Gilbert's voice? It does sound like something out of a Nabokov novel. Dead-Gilbert might have appreciated that. I responded apologetically, explained my mistake, and did not hear from Living-Gilbert again.

Finally, with only the memorial compilation, I contacted CereProc and began an email correspondence with a software developer there, Graham Leary. As an introduction to CereProc, Graham told me about one of his projects that involved making a synthesized voice for Jason Bradbury, a television presenter known for his work on *The Gadget Show*. The voice was used in a robotic model of Bradbury's head and torso. Graham sent me a link to a YouTube video in which Robot-Jase, wearing a bowtie, is introduced as the first robot to host a live UK television broadcast. Standing next to his double, Jason says: "He's the star of the show. I'm like a bit-part. FOR MYSELF. It's very postmodern." Graham disclaimed that the lip-syncing is not very good, and that CereProc did not work on that.

Graham was exactly what I had been looking for: an expert in voice synthesis with a mischievous sense of humour. Without hesitation (or announcement), I cast him as Gilbert in my improvised production of *The Inhuman Voice*.

> James: I've been wanting to ask, what were the mechanics of appropriating ~~Lewis Carroll's~~ Roger Ebert's voice, for example? How did you begin?
>
> Graham-Gilbert: I normally build voices for living subjects, who read from a script in controlled studio conditions. I need around fifty hours of recorded audio of a subject speaking to make a functional voice synthesis. However, as you know, in 2009 CereProc did make a voice for Roger Ebert, after he lost his speech. That voice was built entirely from prerecorded material. We cut each of the recordings into very small fragments that are called "diphones." A diphone is the transition from one phone to another. So, if you take a

word like "cat," the phones are "cuh," "ah," "tuh," and the diphones are "silence-to-cuh," "cuh-to-ah," "ah-to-tuh," and "tuh-to-silence" . . .

Speaking of cats, in *Alice Through the Needle's Eye*, Gilbert's Alice meets Ping and Pang, two Siamese who are joined at the tail and speak as one being, habitually finishing each other's sentences. "You took the very words out of my mouth!"

. . . We cut the recordings into diphones, rather than cutting them into individual phones, because there's less variability in the middle of a phone than there is on a phone boundary. The boundaries are where the most characteristic parts of each phone are found. These cuttings—some as short as one tenth of a second —are then stored in a database. Our software rapidly recombines the cuttings to render the speech. A voice synthesis is programmable in a text-to-speech framework, where text input into any supported software can be spoken aloud by the computer.

James: Are there any other methods for building a voice synthesis?

Graham-Gilbert: There are many. The one I described is CONCATENATIVE voice synthesis. The actual sound from the original recording of the subject speaking is preserved. The synthesis is in the division and recombination of the sounds. One alternative, a FORMANT synthesis, builds an entirely virtual system by modelling the characteristics of a subject's voice and reproducing them digitally.

This distinction between Concatenative and Formant synthesis reminded me of the Deleuze quote I had shared with Gilbert. A Concatenative voice synthesis would reconstitute Gilbert's own words—taken right out of his mouth—yet *monstrously*. Puppet-Gilbert.

Something else Graham said resonated. In the production of a Concatenative voice synthesis for a living subject, there is an automated process for dividing the recording into its constituent diphones. Speech recognition software processes the recording, matching the audio to the script read by the subject. The computer can only process the audio if it recognizes the exact sequence of utterances found in the script.

Ping If it knows what the speaker . . .

Pang . . . will say.

This process is called "forced alignment." The computer is matching what it hears to the basic structure of the script, forcing the recorded sounds into the predetermined rhythm of the text. In the case of a deceased subject—since a dead person cannot read a script—the "script" must be produced after the recording. A transcript of a recording would be given to the computer so that it can perform its forced alignment. These contrary flows, *script* → *speech* alignment and *speech* → *script* alignment circled my attention back to preemptive hoaxes and anticipatory plagiarism. Gilbert would have made the connection, too. In *Love and Death on Long Island*, his disturbed protagonist writes: "My novel flowed as fluently from my pen as though the complete narrative had somehow been miniaturized in advance and injected into the nib and it were merely a matter of posing the pen over the paper, teasing each word, like a droplet of ink, off its tip and having it spill onto the blank page."

Another point of interest on the matter of transcription. There are established orthographies for the representation of phones and diphones, and the stresses on particular sounds in any given articulation of a word. Graham provided examples of phonetic orthography from CereProc's

Received Pronunciation lexicon:

Input k_a1_t
Output Cat.

Input k_a1_t_@0_n_ai0_n_t_ei1_l_z
Output Cat-o'-nine-tails.

Input k_a2_t_@0_k_l_i1_z_m_i0_k
Output Cataclysmic.

The numbers indicate the stress: primary (1), secondary (2) and unstressed (0).

Finally, my conversation with Graham arrived at the decisive question. The memorial compilation is 38 minutes long, but unfortunately includes only around eight minutes of Gilbert speaking that are clearly audible, free from background music or ambient sound.

> James: Is it technically possible to make a Concatenative voice synthesis from only a tiny sample of source material?
>
> Graham-Gilbert: Your material would probably only have partial diaphone coverage. Confronted with a database that lacks certain diphones, there are successive levels of "back-away" that our software would resort to. In the ideal situation, the database would contain all of the possible diphones, and the software would recombine them in the largest available chunks. The software would try to preserve the recorded clusters of sounds as far as possible. If you typed a word like "caution", and the word "cautious" had been recorded in the script, the

software would render the "causha" from the recording and then graft an "n" onto the end from another cutting. It doesn't always concatenate at the diphone level. If the database were missing some particularly obscure diphone—such as sh_ch, zh_ch, or zh_zh—the result might only very occasionally manifest in the rendered speech. The software would substitute the missing diphone with another similar sounding diphone from the same database. In case of a very patchy database, once potential subtitutions were exhausted, the software would be programmed to contact an alternative database, producing an audible slippage in the rendered speech as the software inserts diphones from the secondary source. It would work, but it would sound very odd, like an aural version of a ransom note.

A Robot-Gilbert produced using only these eight minutes of material would be able to speak only a severely limited English, bound by the diphones Gilbert happened to utter in the clips compiled by David Thompson.

GILBERT AGAIN

Gilbert wrote that during the four years that he worked on translating Perec's lipogrammatic prose, his perspective on the constraint changed. "At the outset, the language I had to contend with seemed to me frankly 'crippled,' as though, in losing all its 'e's, it had lost several seriously major limbs. Then, as I started to feel more comfortable with its warped angularities, I became inclined to regard it less as 'crippled' than as 'disabled,' diminished by its loss of limbs, to be sure, but still capable of living a rich and full life."

Depending on the accent of the speaker, spoken English contains 40 to

44 phones. Received Pronunciation English has 44. The number of diphones equals the number of phones squared. There are also diphones between each phone and silence, making the total number 45 × 45 (-1 as silence–silence is not required) = 2024 diphones in Received Pronunciation English. The number of missing diphones in Robot-Gilbert's Concatenative voice synthesis is around a third of these, including some common diphones. Robot-Gilbert's language is DECIDEDLY crippled. Could even Gilbert have mastered such a constraint? Robot-Gilbert is not programmed to use a substitute database in the case of missing diphones, so whenever a diphone he cannot utter or substitute appears in the text, he simply skips over it, without any allowance in timing. As I familiarize myself with his controls, it seems I might have to abandon any idea of writing a sophisticated monologue using all of Robot-Gilbert's diphones. I resort to trial and error, experimenting with the transformative defects of Robot-Gilbert's strange concatenations on text.

Earlier in the process, I had come across an auspicious fragment of dialogue that I hoped would make the perfect conclusion to my exchange with Found-Gilbert. Gilbert co-wrote Portuguese director Raul Ruiz's 1981 film *The Territory*, in which a group of tourists embark on a hiking trip in a vast forest. They employ a guide called Gilbert. Guide-Gilbert's motivations are unclear, but during the first day of their expedition, the group begin to doubt him. "He's leading us in circles," one of the group protests, as they pass the same few landmarks repeatedly. That night at their campsite an argument ensues, and Guide-Gilbert abandons the group. Days later they are still lost, their efforts to find a way out of the forest increasingly desperate.

"Did you walk in a straight line?"

"I tried to but it's impossible."

"Maybe we should try walking in circles if we want to go in a straight line."

Delirious, they stumble upon Guide-Gilbert's body, his death unexplained. The discovery forces a terrible decision. Cannibalism might be their only option for survival. Objectifying the body helps the group to rationalize their actions: "Why do we still call him Gilbert? He's just a corpse now." The meat is cooked and passed around. As the adults eat with grim faces, two boys playfully argue over the provenance of the meat. One says to the other: "This is Gilbert, not your Gilbert." The other replies: "I've got a better piece than you. It's more Gilbert than your Gilbert."

Let me introduce Robot-Gilbert with a demonstration. I type this last line of dialog into TextEdit, in phonetic code. Missing the diphone b _@0, Robot-Gilbert can't resist treading on his Master's toes:

James: i1_t–_s m_oo1 g_i1_l_b_@0_t dh_@0_n y_oo1 g_i1_l_b_@0_t

Robot-Gilbert: It's more Gilbot than your Gilbot.

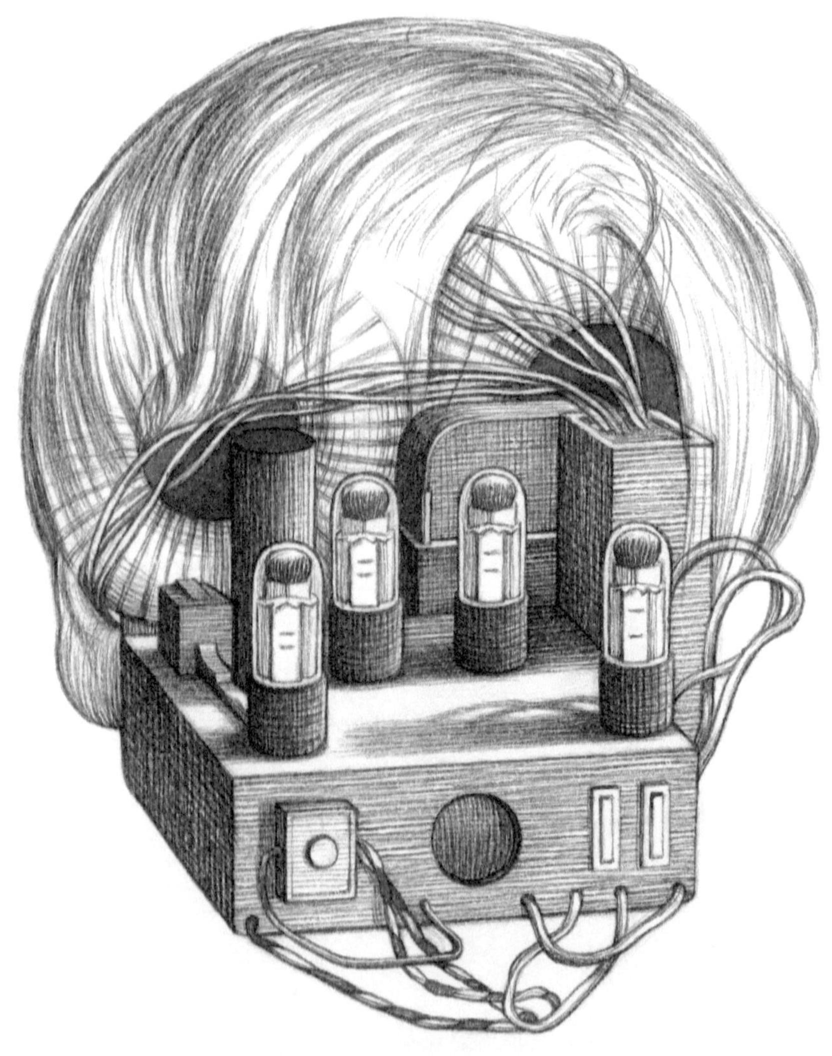

This is Not a Second Novel

M.J. NICHOLLS

1

A phalanx of salmon escalopes, fretted with feta on twelve piebald plates, met the tuxedoed frame of B.S. Johnson scholar Kris Valvanetti as I parted the louvre doors and received him with a booming welcome: "OH, FUCK ALL THIS LYSINE!" I shook his limp hand and admired his shirt cuffs, extra-ruffled in homage to the famous photo of B.S. holding his unbound novel *The Unfortunates*, and introduced him to Linda. "Is this your latest acquisition?" he asked. "His latest hagquisition," Linda replied. Kris shook her hand and took a second to process the pun. "Smashing!" I was throwing a shindig in celebration of my first novel, *The House of Writers*, a satire that had sent an exocet missile into the heart of the literary establishment, to paraphrase Chester Horton in *The Guardian*, and earned me enough to purchase a small cottage in Bridge of Weir, a popular semi-rural burrow for nouveau riche Scots and English retirees with pension pots too small for the Highlands. "I hope to avoid an aposiopesis this evening!" Kris quipped. I smiled knowingly, having read *Albert Angelo* from which that word and my opening line derived, and pointed him towards the escalopes, which he probed like a ravenous man not ravenous enough to eat his most hated food. Further invitees trickled into the cottage: Fiona Gregor, an Ann Quin scholar from Saltcoats who spent the evening staring at the carpet and fingering the reprint of *Berg* in my bookcase; Vernon Eventual, a sci-fi writer with nine unpublished novels in the drawer who elected himself head of the Renfrewshire SF Council (at present with nine functioning members); Iris Compox, a scriptwriter for BBC3 comedies whose sardonic poseur and fondness for the flat one-liner sent people rushing to hide in the toilet; Harriet Staidnose, an aficionado of the rare words dictionary, whose casual use of archaisms forced listeners to question and endure her flawlessly memorised definitions; J. Adam Botwell, a hip scholar who had co-edited a new William Burroughs Reader with fresh cut-up material acquired during an illegal raid on Burroughs's archives; Silvia Mild, a florid mother-of-nine who boasted about having read the complete works of Joyce Carol Oates; Driscoll Flapper, whose comparative exegesis of the works of Paul and Alexander Theroux was three-starred in the *Miami Book Bunker*; Arnold Brightchin, author of the thimble novel *Chirp*, winner of the Blake Butler Prize For Barely Tolerable Innovation and readable only with a magnifying glass; Holly Slalom, a PhD student organising a conference on the role of metamorphosis in the Albanian novel; Bo Henry, writing a self-reflexive thing about his almost namesake O. Henry, and his failure to appreciate a single of O.'s stories; Callum Broker, an accountant who had read two Chuck Palahnuik novels in his lifetime and was eager to discuss them at length with anyone in the vicinity; among others too numerous and uninvited to name.

2

As the escalopes vanished and the inexpensive non-alcoholic sparkling wine substitute dwindled to a drip, the conversation turned to me, and what I might elect to write about for that difficult second novel.

"You have Carte D'or blanche, dear fellow, second novels are fated to obscurity," Kris Valvanetti said. Not thinking to add that B.S. Johnson's first novel *Travelling People* had been suppressed and forgotten while his second is known among those in the know. I read the answer in his eyes: "That was the author's *choice*."

"In the case of Burroughs," J. Adam Botwell said, "the notorious *Naked*

Lunch was the Beatitude of the Beats. And later, his true second novel, *Queer*, also sizzled on the pan of success and warmed trangressive cockles."

"Do you *speak* in cut-ups?" Iris Compox said.

"Ann Quin's second novel is *Three*," Fiona Gregor said. No one heard her because she spoke into her cup beside the bookcase, where the copy of *Berg* found itself sniffed and inhaled with loving mania.

"You should write a 3000-page epic, like SF writer Arnold F. Milwell. An inflated folly that fails totally, and is near unreadable, but contains the most radical failed experimentation imaginable in your nodes. Arnold's novel, *The Intergalactic Supernovae*, is 3281 pages, published in three volumes, with a separate volume for footnotes and explanatory material. Inflated failure is better than lithe triumph. Blitz the reader with small fonts, incoherent concepts, ceaseless sentences, and hair-pulling dialogue," Vernon Eventual said.

"Like *Infinite Jest*?" Iris asked.

"You have a swarm of janissaries," Harriet Staidnose said, "you may as well write a lexiphanicistic *künstlerroman*."

"That's what I said," Vernon said.

"Paul Theroux wrote *Fong and the Indians*," Driscoll Flapper said, "featuring a Chinese storekeeper in East Africa. Alexander Theroux wrote *Darconville's Cat*, one of the TOWERING MASTERPIECES OF THE 20TH CENTURY (caps deliberate)."

"Am I detecting a bias?" I asked.

"You can't *speak* in caps," Iris said.

"O. Henry never wrote a novel," was the last thing Bo Henry said that evening.

"I remember first reading Joyce Carol Oates's second novel, back when I was a teenager," Silvia Mind said. "*A Garden of Earthly Delights*. About—"

"—a young woman struggling with a patriarchal upbringing in the American midwest?" Iris interjasked.

"Yes. How did you know?"

"I think I might write about a shepherd with diabetes who learns to appreciate the kindness of obese left-wing comedians," I said.

"Bestseller in the making!" Iris again.

"Can I say something about Chuck Palahnuik's second novel *Invisible Monsters*?" Callum Broker asked.

"Yeah, what?" someone replied.

"I've read it. Have any of you guys?"

"No!" you guys replied.

This colloquy continued into the weeest of the wee hours, that is 4.59AM, the weeest by virtue of being the furthest into the night before dawn dittoed at 5AM, during which we debated whether the word 'weeest' should have a hyphen between the second and third e's to help the reader to easier catch its meaning, a debate spoiled by a drunk Holly Slalom, whose invective against the participants of her unstaged conference reached libellous levels, and whose tattoos of former Yugoslav diplomats on her clavicle spoiled the upbeat atmosphere created by lively banter on my future works. People exited with the sour expressions of cabinet ministers leaving photo ops in London pubs.

3

Over an unbuttered brioche, as I ambled around the living room, standing at one point on the Ann Quin scholar, passed out beside the bookcase having licked the spine from *Berg* down to the adhesive, I decided the second novel should be a bittersweet exploration of my first failed long-term relationship in the form of a writer failing to write a bittersweet exploration of his first failed long-term relationship, making use of the reliable technique of self-aware recursion, a technique I have reused recursively in a self-aware manner for years. I would simultaneously mine literary riches from and emotionally address this eight-year relationship while ruminating on the business of writing second novels. I would contrast my current relationship with Linda to my first with Name Redacted, and contrive some link between the ongoing second novel and my first, making the despairing point that although things might seem refreshingly fresh (in a new relationship and a new novel), the same failure is inevitable, because human behaviour and my novels are recursive things, and so fated to the same doomed outcomes.

Two days after the breakup, I had opened a Word file entitled *A Sentimental Document*, in which I intended to commemorate everything I loved about my ex-girlfriend, committing the memories to paper before time swiped them, with the intention of sending this to her as a means of achieving what is sought in the nauseating idiom 'closure'. I was advised by my ex-girlfriend's mother this was a bad idea, partly to prevent me from sending a melodramatic screed of drivel and embarrassing myself, partly to uphold my ex-girlfriend's "no contact indefinitely" policy, meaning a response to such a document would never arrive, nor would the document probably be read in light of a final hysterical email sent as the last in a series of one-way correspondences. I mused on respectable literary ways in which I could use this emotionally upsetting experience in a manner that would also fulfil my sitcommercial desire for 'closure'—a false form of restitution for unsatisfying events, required to help delude you into thinking one string-quartet-soundtracked moment might bring forth inner peace, when in life events merely trickle, fizzle, and peter out, and satisfying resolutions are in the end subbed in favour of hardcore forgetting. I would never, unless I chose to keep a private collection of written memories for repeated nostalgic torture upon their discovery (I am convinced all nostalgia is a form of self-torture, urging you to recall long-buried events and their miserable outcomes in a perpetual loop), commemorate the relationship with specific references to actual events, and loving signals to the ex-girlfriend, whose friendship I still desired at the end, and for whom my affection remained stubbornly undimmed, despite her rather bluntly forbidding communication, with only the promise of a friendly greeting should our paths ever cross again accidentally, and that to write such a work would be to preserve a still relatively recent point of view, meaning that at some point in the future, having had no contact for many years, my heart may have utterly hardened towards her, solidified somehow by the long forced exile, and that a potentially unread encomium of a person who spurned me may prove embarrassing at a later date. Leaving the only course of action to write nothing at all, or to write something like this paragraph.

4

A shameless showcase of leashslipped ambition or a lean validation of my talents? *Infinite Jest* or *The Crying of Lot 49*? I tickled the options. First, I would avoid the Ralph Ellison curse of never producing a second novel, leaving behind a paper chase of hopeless and muddled drafts. I would avoid this since I hadn't written a first novel on a par with *Invisible Man* and hadn't secured the same financial success as Ellison. I hadn't the patience (or intelligence) to write an epic on a par with *Darconville's Cat* or *The Tunnel*, so I was looking at a shorter, or similar-length novel. The possibilities were vast. Ballard imagines a flooded planet besieged by tropical temperatures and reversion to primitive living in *The Drowned World*; Russell Hoban describes in *Kleinzeit* a copywriter with a skewed hypotenuse in a novel where God, the Hospital, and the Word narrate the tale; Nicholson Baker rocks his child to sleep for 20 minutes and logs the minutiae of his thoughts in under 120 pages in *Room Temperature*; Flann O'Brien imagines a vision of Hell in rural Ireland where bike-obsessed policemen preside over the mysteries of the universe in *The Third Policeman*; Will Self in *Great Apes* imagines a reverse Planet of the Apes scenario, where an artist awakes to a world populated by primates; George Orwell delivers in *A Clergyman's Daughter* a powerful putdown of English private schools and their spirals of hopeless corruption. And me? I could narrate the tale of a woman trapped in a paedophile's mobile phone, and her conflict between trying to escape, and outing the monster to the police. A stalled rollercoaster becomes the setting for a heated eschatological colloquium and when the ride resumes the swift plummet into darkness has horrifying repercussions. Two Chinese students accept unpaid work tasting lemon curd. A romance novelist sells her unpublished first draft on Ebay for £90. Three cinephiles make their own film but having seen the final edit, refuse to show up to the premiere. I tickled these choices for weeks, until they begged me to stop.

5

"It seems to me," said the man behind the counter in a Bridge of Weir cornershop whose name was Lionel Avast, "that there is no one story in particular that would keep you rapt enough to fatten a folio."

"Explain, Lionel?"

"It seems to me, and I am a mere man in a corner shop, that with your incessant listing of plots, ideas, sketches, and speculative fumbling, you are condemning yourself to the unpopular art of digression."

"Explain, Lionel?"

"It seems to me, and pardon these repetitions, that these lists bespeak of a weariness around the writing act. You are blasé about executing an idea in usual or unusual forms. You are a drunken moth making an unsuccessful flutter towards the lamp, landing with worn wings in the cold minestrone."

"Explain, Lionel?"

"It seems to me, and I seem to seem loads, that no simple elegant novels will pirouette from your fingertips, and that blasé bursts of huff-and-puff weirdness are the future of you. A Mini Cooper in perpetual stall is the car you drive."

"Explain, Lionel?"

"It seems to me, and I am coming apart at the seems, that self-mulling fictions are your trade in socks. You walk in ill-fitting shoes, your ambidextrous feet guide you towards dead-ends, and you masturbate there, in bliss."

"Explain, Lionel?"

"It seems to me that you aren't going to buy that Twix, are you?"

"Explain, Lionel?"

"Please leave my shop."

6

This is not a second novel. There will be no second novel. There will be no more novels. There will be no more reheated plots and packaged characters. No more microwave thrillers. Boil-in-the-bag romances. No more virtuoso showcases of an MFA-stamped prose in the *Upcoming Whelps Quarterly*. No more workshops with pens being twirled and chins being stroked. No more earnest feedback on lumpen prose and overwrought poems. Fiction on the ooze. Strangers with nine novels in them begging to be expressed. Pastel colours and sunsets and women with blank expressions staring into the middle distance on all book covers until Christendom. There will be no more novels until the backlog is dealt with. The relentless pummelling of transient fictions on a casual readership. The seasonal sainted book and its author retreating to their bucolic nook to pen a forgotten second. The million manuscripts on the desk of A.P. Rose Associates and the two interns skimming them for movie potential. Retired businessmen settling down to pursue literary success. Nineteen-year-old emos self-publishing *The Darkness is Rising III: Darkness Begets Darkness*. There will be no more novels. There will be only apologies. Reader, I am sorry for this novel you are holding in your hands. I simply have no other means of expression and I desperately need an outlet. Reader, maximum apologies! I know this novel does not need to exist. I have toiled at this for three years, so you understand I had to publish! And on the front cover of future bestsellers: YOU DO NOT *NEED* TO READ THIS. HAVE YOU CONSIDERED SOMETHING FROM ANOTHER DECADE? HAVE YOU EVER SPARED A THOUGHT FOR THE AUTHOR WITHOUT MASS COMMERCIAL BACKING, YOU POPULIST WHORE? MIGHT YOU LOOK AT LITERARY TRANSLATIONS? SMALL PRESS BOOKS? PERHAPS IF YOU COULD CEASE FOLLOWING THE HERD FOR THREE MINUTES, YOU MAY DISCOVER A WORLD OF LITERATURE MORE SUITED TO THE INTELLIGENT YOU LURKING SOMEWHERE BELOW? My future, my kingdom for a dream.

The Strange History of Clarence Major's All-Night Visitors

KEITH BYERMAN

Clarence Major has a long and distinguished career as a novelist, poet, and painter. Though less well-known than other members of his generation of African-American writers (Toni Morrison, Alice Walker, Charles Johnson, John Edgar Wideman), Major can be seen as the most experimental of the group. He was a member for several years of the Fiction Collective and engaged in many of the same challenges to mainstream narrative forms. His first novel, *All-Night Visitors* (1969), is typical of his work: it jumps around in time and place; its narrator is problematic; it calls attention to itself as a fiction; it shifts discursive registers, often within a paragraph; it is exuberantly sexually explicit. Then, thirty years later (1998), much of what made the novel so important to Major's reputation was repudiated with the publication of an "unexpurgated edition" of the book, with an introduction by Bernard Bell. This version not only restored some of the (nonsexual) material that Major claims the publisher wanted deleted, but it added new material that was not in either the first edition nor an edited typescript that preceded that version.[1] The end result is a work that is more "literary" but also less innovative. The focus of this article is on the radical nature of the 1969 edition and the subsequent neutralizing of some of those effects. The ultimate question I hope to engage through this discussion is what we

---

1   See Byerman, for a brief description of the publishing history of the novel.

mean by "experimental" in a situation in which the author has an opportunity to revise an early work in a manner that can redefine his/her career. If future readers have primary access to the "restored" text, in what ways will they define Major as an experimental writer?

All-Night Visitors, given its sources, was bound to be a nontraditional text. Rather than the product of a unitary concept, no matter how complex, it instead grew out of disparate failed attempts at writing novels. Major had unfinished manuscripts on Vietnam, the Lower East Side of New York, Chicago, and an orphanage. He had not been able to make any of them work, but instead of discarding them, he took fragments of each one, gave them a common first-person narrator, and turned them into what he called an "epic collage poem."[2] He was unable to find a mainstream or even independent house interested in publishing it. In desperation, he turned to Maurice Girodias, whose Olympia Press focused on pornographic works, though it worked with some avant-garde authors, such as J.P. Donleavy. Girodias wanted more emphasis on the erotic material. To meet this demand, Major cut the novel, but also, apparently because he felt his original vision was lost, randomized the chapters. The result was even more of a "collage" than he had originally planned; arbitrary juxtaposition of material from the various manuscripts destroyed all sense of continuity, cause and effect, and character development. For example, the second chapter of the book focuses on the departure of the key female character Cathy, an event that appears to have a crucial effect on the narrator, Eli Bolton. But then she disappears until the fourteenth chapter, where she is introduced and given a personal history. In the penultimate chapter of the book, we learn of her sexual problems, including the abuse she suffered from her stepfather.

The revisions for Girodias also draw attention to matters of style. Not surprisingly, much of the verbal innovation has to do with sexuality. In the first chapter ("Tammy"), which focuses on Eli's intercourse with a character whose name appears only once elsewhere in the novel, he gives us twenty-four different terms for his penis. A few of these provide the

---

2   "How *All-Night Visitors* Was Made," *Nickel Review*, 3, no. 1 (April 1969), p. 11.

limited humor the text contains: Mr. Ill-Bred, Mr. Perpendicular, supernatural enravisher, Mr. Rooster. By comparison, the words for female genitalia are both less numerous and more conventional; they are precisely the ones we would expect in a more or less pornographic text. Where the exuberance also appears is in his names for Cathy; in the penultimate chapter, he offers forty-two variations on her name, eight in one sentence: "I knew well this psychology and often studied waitresses but not now, they didn't exist, nobody but Cathea, glorious Kathi, gentle Caathy, sacred Katheas, my empress, Cato Katheus, my princess, Catti my whore, divine Kathee, my angel Cathela!" (187).

These separate but parallel acts of extravagant naming have the effect of eroticizing the text regardless of what they signify. They call attention to the author's verbal playfulness far beyond any narrative necessity. He creates virtually a new language as part of the construction of his text. This play effectively subverts any sense of a novel that serves a social or mimetic purpose. Specifically, Major is consciously rejecting the notion that art by African-American writers functions primarily as a means of advancing a racial agenda. That argument had been made virtually since the beginning of black literature and was receiving renewed defense at the time *All-Night Visitors* was first published with the emergence of the Black Arts Movement. Like many young artists before him, Major refused to write to any ideological formula.

But he goes further than most in doing so. It is not accidental that his two main verbal displays involve his narrator's genitalia and the identity of a young white woman. Black manhood and white womanhood have been linked in the American psyche since the early days of slavery. Rather than evade or euphemize this national taboo, Major makes it the central subject of his text. From the first chapter to virtually the last, Eli describes in graphic detail his sexual activities, especially with white women. Moreover, he defines his own identity in such terms: "My dick is my life, it has to be" (4). Moreover, the text reveals little sense of guilt or social threat in these interactions. Eli moves from woman to woman, concerned only that they do what he wants; he only seems to have difficulties when they act contrary to his wishes or he becomes bored with them. White males on rare occasions seem troubled by the relationships, but they fail to act.

But the novel should not be mistaken as a celebration of sexuality in the tradition of Henry Miller or Anais Nin, two of the influences on Major's early career. Accompanying the eroticism is a strong, almost equal focus on violence. It is here that Major introduces a third element (after narrative fracturing and sexuality) of innovation. Violence in and of itself is not, of course, necessarily experimental. Many strands of conventional writing make use of it: realism and naturalism, romanticism, gothic narrative, genre literature. What is distinctive in *All-Night Visitors* is its close association with sexuality and the narrator. The gang-killing of an old man, the sadistic hanging of a dog in the orphanage, the rape and murder of Vietnamese children by American soldiers are not innovative in modern fiction. In these instances, in fact, Major is largely working in the naturalist tradition going back to Theodore Dreiser and Frank Norris and continuing in the Richard Wright school of black narrative.

What marks the difference is Eli Bolton's narcissism and callousness toward women that allows him to commit both psychological and physical abuse. It is important to note that he is not some variation on a Poe madman-narrator who is driven by a loss of reason to acts of murder. Rather, he is the id, who seeks nothing but the fulfillment of desires, and responds strongly to any frustration of that desire. He says in the first paragraph of the novel: "All I want her for is to fuck her. She is hardly worth anything else" (3). His impulse is not limited by the fact that his behavior borders on pedophilia: "She is nude beneath the sheet, I know. I pull it all the way down, and stroke her little girl-size body. Each tit is no bigger than half an orange . . ." (5). Nor do her own problems concern him: "I turn her little white wrists over and look at them. They are healing, where she cut them with the coke bottle that first night here" (5). "I want to fuck her like she is a *thing*. I don't want to see her eyes when I screw her, because sometimes they are *too* sad" (5). He refuses involvement in her humanity because it will disrupt his focus on himself.

To make her "pay" for making an implicit claim on his life, he forces her into an act of fellatio, during which he deliberately delays his own orgasm in order to make her work almost to exhaustion to satisfy him.

The more significant act, however, is directed against Cathy in the second chapter. Because she is leaving, he contemplates murder:

> Yes; I'll kill her.
>
> To keep her with me, I'll eat her flesh and do it very slowly, so she will last, so in my silent hysterical (though you may say psychiatric) desolation I'll have the comfort of her, now in this unworshipping loveless world. (17)

He then remembers a moment when he wanted to snap off her fingers, one by one and imagines that she would thank him for destroying "the phallic symbols of myself that I've been so frightened of all my life . . ." (19).

What in fact he does is rape her on the street as she attempts to leave. It is a scene over three pages long and thus comparable to the pleasurable scenes elsewhere in the book. The difference is that this one blends realistic and surrealistic elements: he describes members of a Puerto Rican gang beating an old man and also goes off on an extended imagistic stream of consciousness:

> And though the rudimentary hour of the morning seems inflammable with the electric fact that this street, like every other one of them crossing our nerves at this moment, is a cheap *bolo* bitching stretch of psychic cement, paved blind to our social emergency! The ghosts thrilling and voltaic in their natural but painstaking eternal money-dance here, accept us, Cathy, the whitest, holy constituent of this latitude of the earth—trembling! suddenly! A stranger,

> beneath my classic and graceful rape . . . (25)

What Bolton comments on in Cathy's response is not so much her fear and pain, but rather her identity as a white woman. As he enacts the stereotypic role of the black beast attacking white womanhood, he comments on the racial nature of the moment. But his language, as seen above, does not fit the racist image of the black man who has no control over his behavior; instead, he performs the role self-consciously and deliberately.

This self-awareness in combination with the rhetorical flourishes is perhaps the most radical gesture of the 1969 version. Major defies the whole tradition of black writing by making the rapist the center of narrative consciousness; he is given the chance to justify behavior that is taboo in American society. Moreover, by embedding the rape in the context of other criminal activity and surreal language, he both emphasizes and distracts from its centrality. Since this is a narrator who repeatedly seeks our understanding, Major challenges the reader to define the limits of acceptable narration. After all, this scene occurs in the second chapter of the novel. We are asked to stay with and even sympathize with Bolton through the rest of his story.

The version of the novel published three decades later rearranges, deletes, and adds material, including elements that did not appear in the typescript or the 1969 edition. While most of the sexual scenes remain, they are contextualized by background information and, on occasion, subsequent nonsexual events. The structure is profoundly altered. The chapters (except for "Tammy" as the opening) are organized chronologically, with new family history material leading to the experiences in the orphanage, followed by the Vietnam chapters, then life in Chicago, and concluding with events on New York's Lower East Side. The net effect is a more or less conventionally-told fictional autobiography, with a narrator/central character who we come to know in the traditional way, through sequential story-telling that creates the impression of cause and effect. The linguistic extravagances remain, but they lost some of their power through the predominance of a more or less realistic narration.

Notably missing is the rape scene, though the misogyny of the rest of the text remains. The deletion of this event and the movement of the remainder of that chapter to near the end of the book gives an entirely different sense of the narrator. He is no longer personally violent (he does admit to having killed in Vietnam). The addition of a set of chapters about his life with Cathy in Chicago and New York provides a context that turns his response of violence to one of sorrow.

The inclusion of those chapters also adds a level of social commentary that had not previously been present. They are mostly surreal, suggesting an apocalypse involving the Second Coming; but instead of Christ, a tarbaby parachutes to earth. The sequence is televised with a black reporter named Buckwheat and a white one named Jack Beanstalk. This section takes on qualities associated with Ralph Ellison (who briefly appears as a character) and Ishmael Reed, whose experimental fiction started being published shortly before Major's. Several of the characters from previous sections of the book are parodied in their interviews with Buckwheat and Beanstalk. Slapstick is incorporated as Bolton keeps spilling odd objects from his suitcase. It is the most extended humorous sequence in either version of the novel.

So what, finally, are we to make of such distinct versions of this experimental work? The first point I would make is that by 1998 Major was in the process of trying to consolidate his reputation as an artist. He published a career-long collection of his poetry in 1999 and a book of essays in 2000; he largely stopped writing long fiction, with only one novel after 1998; and Bernard Bell edited a collection of criticism on him in 2001. He was also an active participant in the writing of a biography that came out in 2012. In this context, the revision of *All-Night Visitors* can be seen as another effort to define his career in his own terms. He produced a text over which he had complete control.

It is also the case that his definition of "experimental" has changed over time; this can be seen in his poetry and painting as well as his fiction.

Whereas the early novels, written at the height of Sixties and Seventies radical innovation, much of more recent fiction, even that he labels experimental, uses many of the traditional devices of fiction. By "restoring" *All-Night Visitors* to something close to the narrative he originally constructed, he has in fact made it more acceptable to a new audience. The kinds of nonconventional elements, such as parody and surrealism, employed in the 1998 version have proved to have more staying power than those he felt compelled to employ in 1969. Moreover, the deletion of material such as the rape scene makes it a work better attuned to a current readership, including women and a new generation of African-American writers and readers accustomed to authors such as Percival Everett and Colson Whitehead.

Each edition, then, is a kind of historical object, created out of the conditions of particular literary and social moments and, whether intentionally or not, speaking to those moments. The sexual revolution, feminist movement, metafiction, and assertion of strong black male identity of the post civil rights period was followed a postfeminist, "post-soul" era. The two versions of the novel can almost be read as completely different works, each "experimental" in the terms permitted by the moment of creation. So, in this sense Major remains true to his innovative impulses and artistic ambitions.

Works Cited

Bell, Bernard W. *Clarence Major and His Art: Portraits of an African American Postmodernist*. Chapel Hill: University of North Carolina Press, 2001.
Byerman, Keith. *The Art and Life of Clarence Major*. Athens: University of Georgia Press, 2012.
Major, Clarence. *All-Night Visitors*. New York: Olympia Press, 1969.
-------. *All-Night Visitors*. Foreword by Bernard W. Bell. Boston: Northeastern University Press, 1998.
-------. "How *All-Night Visitors* Was Made," *Nickel Review*, 3, no. 1 (April 1969), p. 11.

On Katrina Palmer's The Dark Object

PETER BLUNDELL

A colleague of mine on an undergraduate Surface Textile course recently told of a project brief she had been given to create a response to the Olympic 2012 legacy in London. The project required her not to make an outcome in media (presumably textile-based) but rather to anticipate or 'visualize' its existence.

She was in effect asked to propose hypothetically, through drawings and written-form, the physical nature of the outcome. The brief requiring her to describe in detail the materials used, processes involved, as well as indicating how the resultant outcome fed by her research would be presented. The central protagonist in Katrina Palmer's darkly-comic debut novel *The Dark Object* finds himself in a similar predicament albeit with far more dramatic and sinister circumstances.

In Palmer's story, Addison Cole is the lone student at *The School of Sculpture Without Objects*. A strange establishment in which the making of objects is forbidden. We find the student locked in a room with only a computer, chairs and tables to speak of, the studio being nothing more than a neglected office space. Seeking some kind of consolation, Cole conjures up ever-fantastical encounters with individuals and objects.

These encounters become increasingly charged with an overt physicality, the flow of which overspill into the central narrative frame of *The Dark Object* before being interrupted by incoming email messages from the Rector, the school's authority. Near the beginning of the book we hear the Rector tell the Secretary "get that student into the studio, lock the door, make sure there's no way of escape." From this point on, Cole receives frequent messages such as: "Student, please supply an eight hundred word abstract of your project" to which Cole bemuses: "abstract of what?"

Cole is subjected to an extreme form of conceptual pedagogy that seeks to remove art from form: "There must be no object!" the rector declares. The tendency in art terms referred to as 'dematerialization' in which the shadow of Marcel Duchamp is cast over generations of artists from the late-sixties onwards is a heavily-trodden path of academic writing on art. Palmer is aware of this, as well as with the more contemporary conditions of dematerialization primarily stemming from the digital realm and the stark economic realities that any number cash-strapped art institutions face.

By placing this now familiar critique in fictional form, Palmer is seeking to "fabricate objects in the writing" and in turn expand the possibility of fiction.[1] Echoes of Kafka and Beckett resound in the corridors and neglected office spaces of *The School of Sculpture Without Objects* as does the Russian-doll, story within story structure of Flann O'Brien's *At Swim-Two-Birds.*

What marks *The Dark Object* out from the fray is the sheer anarchic acceleration of the prose, its twists and turns that propel the symbolic thrust. We, the reader, are literally thrown into scenarios both absurd and alienating but always configured in support of a singular vision of writing. Palmer has carefully drawn these fictional spaces into strata based on the form of an irregular sphere; the idea being that the reader passes from its external surface (main narrative set in the school), through an intermediate layer (imagined scenarios) towards the core (Cole's existential self) and back out again towards the surface.

The Dark Object was to a large extent built from Palmer's doctoral thesis and its accompanying exhibition *Reality Flickers: Writing with Found Objects and Imagined Sculpture* involved in part Palmer reading out passages to individual visitors alone in a room. Initially a strategy to complicate the conventions of academic writing, the narrative form has since been adopted to make the writing itself an artwork before taking on book form.

Indeed *The Dark Object* retains much of the remnants of academic writing, in a similar manner to Robert Musil's *A Man without Qualities* with its essay-style chapter headings and character's espousing thoughts like lecturers but in this case specifically about what constitutes a sculptural object. In 'Diagram' towards the end of the book, Cole comes close to leaving the books central narrative (external layer) and taking us the reader to one side to explain the structure and purpose of the book.

There are also sections of a non-fictional nature that support the narrative whilst appearing not to be a part: 'Rooms and Furnishing Inspection Reports' is a good example. Not only as a nod to the writings of artist Donald Judd's descriptive language of art, but perhaps drawing again on Flann O'Brien's use of cut and paste assemblage within the novel form.

The inspection report is simply an inventory of all the objects in the room from the state and condition of the walls, to the furnishing and air conditioning system. One list appears for the studio, another for the lecture theatre. The inventory acts as counterpoint to the fantastical scenarios that Addison Cole plays out in his mind. Their formal nature only adding to heighten the intensity of the events unfolding within their respective locations. Palmer chooses to focus on these elements separately, giving each chapter its distinction, so as readers we're building a gradual picture.

The assemblage-like structure of the book adds to the oppressive bureaucratic atmosphere. As well as mapping the topography of the school, the scene is inevitably set for crazy situations to unfold. We almost feel Cole reading these reports over to himself, savoring all material descriptions as a further outlet for not being allowed to make an object and express himself physically. Cole is never quite the artist-hero battling against oppression, the romantic image thwarted by the essential absurdity that Palmer is constantly testing us with; *daring us to enter the fictional space.*

In one key episode midway through the book entitled 'Chair-bed' that Palmer herself has performed as a live reading in a gallery context; a male spectator (Cole?) instructs a woman called Carole to perform sexual maneuvers with a chair that turns into a bed. The metamorphosis is played out on many levels: chair turns into bed, along with the woman's body turning into an object. The male instructor has his way with the woman whilst she is entangled in this transition of form completing as it were the symbolic cycle of objectification.

The episode flips when Carole turns to Cole and us the reader (from interior to exterior surface layer) pointing out that this encounter is not only fiction, but she herself is a fiction and this is her own private fantasy. She is in control of the narrative that her fictional self is enveloped in and is now writing it all down to physically reclaim it back from the male instructor. Next to the 'Diagram' chapter previously discussed, this is the most reflexive part of the book, where, as readers we are confronted with the question of who is in control.

Carole is drawn, like many of the characters in *The Dark Object* from actual figures whom Palmer's admires artistically and theoretically. In this case, the performance artist Carolee Schneeman whose work has involved extracting texts from her own body in order to bridge somehow, the gulf between internal mind and external anatomy. In *The Dark Object* Carole does the reverse of the real Carolee Schneeman and once finished writing out the fantasy she rolls up the paper and inserts the text back into herself, the male instructor watching on in horror utters that she is insane but nevertheless wants to know what has been written. Carole refuses; she is not going to tell because it is not for him.

Perhaps the most absurdly comic scenario in the book is reached when Cole is invited to nominate an individual with whom he would have a tutorial. His wish is granted in the 'decaying hollow-eyed skeleton' of the philosopher G.W. Hegel. In this bizarre exchange, the deceased but vocal philosopher amusingly lectures Cole on the merits of mind over matter whilst seated in his studio as a skeleton. The encounter reaches its climax when Hegel reaches for Cole's knee with his 'cold ivory hand' whilst discussing the nature of desire before the student reminds him of the school's policy of prohibiting physical contact.

At the book's conclusion Addison Cole is expected to produce 'something' for his final show, the anticipation builds, the student is controversially proposing to exhibit an object which is of course is forbidden. His expressed provocation sending shockwaves back to the Rector's office. Cole imagines the message acting as a trigger for the Rector to seduce his secretary over the office desk in a fit of paranoid excitement.

With no access to materials Cole begins to play with the office chairs creating a barrier structure or blockade around himself and in the process suffers a slight head wound. In a passage reminiscent of Samuel Beckett's *Ill Seen Ill Said*, from within the womb-like confinement he has built, Cole is reduced to a pathetic voice. A voice bemoaning at length about the pain in his head as a measure of his existential plight until an unknown figure bizarrely reaches into his little blockade and offers him a piece of fruit.

As well as being a satire on art education and an attempt for sculpture to exist in writing, the irony is not lost on the fact that this is a physical book: an increasingly-obsolete form as any art object—doomed to its own dematerialization within the sphere of digital publishing. However, as far as I understand at the time of writing: *The Dark Object* is not available as an ebook.

Notes:

1 Katrina Palmer interviewed by Richard Marshall for *3:AM Magazine* (2010).

The Project of Ruin Value

JOHN TREFRY

*A*t the midpoint of my average life, concurrent with both my trip to *Pedernales Falls and my move to Lawrence, Kansas, a great sense of peace filtered into my reflections on death. So strongly did that revelatory afternoon at Pedernales Falls seem to center me, at that time realizing I would be moving to Kansas, that I spoke, to anyone who would listen, about how the cross-axes between my former homes in Boston, Atlanta, Los Angeles, and Eugene intersected within an hour's drive from Lawrence, with a warm envelopment, a lack of fear, characterizing my being sucked into the earth in the center of the continent, in the center of my past, paralyzed in so many different ways, to live out the rest of my life with nowhere to go. Death was far away, aged thirty-six, arriving in Kansas finally, and abstract in its symmetry.* Δ **This moment a likely cleft or reveal in the diagram of my life that connects me back to sensations of afternoons alone in my family's house, prior to that, days at home with my mother and sister, and to days hence, in retirement at home with my wife, seeing myself completing this writing project that is my adulthood.** *Although I describe it as peace, it was peace within the absurd mathematics of actuary science. It was not peace with the elision, after "Time withdraws from the body," of this particular series of causal years and geographies. Over the event horizon of years into Kansas I've grown into that peace such that mathematics fell out of its contingent role in my reflections. That elision is just fine as it is, without the calming taper of time. Time has tapered, all within that taper is this constellation, refining itself until it cannot refine any further, without center, more time brings only the fortune to, at some point within it, grow to crave the freedom of its end, hope to be born* *again into death with the wherewithal to comprehend that movement, that sinking elision, for a fraction of an instant.*

Three distinct bodies of writing comprise this text you are reading. The Δ *first , written in 2005, primarily in Atlanta's Marriott Marquis, concerns a failed architectural endeavor, significantly under the influence of the first volume of Roubaud's project, "The Great Fire of London," a luminous plasma that birthed its own failure and also maintained the failure long enough for it to expire and leave a never-occupied ruin. This architectural project, unlike Roubaud's dream of the great fire of London which is surrogated by, forever killed by, the project, was actually completed as a work of represenational architecture in 2012, in Eugene, Oregon, rendering the writing a true ruin, abandoned, not staged as such with Speerian forethought. The* Δ **second** *, written in 2012, in an airplane en route to Eugene, in the midst of reading "The Loop", concerns my visit to a place called Pedernales Falls, outside of Austin, Texas, which I had only previously visited prenatally thirty-six years prior on the United States' bicentennial weekend. The final contribution is being written now in 2015, in Lawrence, Kansas, and although I am now a morning person, like Roubaud, this particular segment materializing under the cone of light containing my armchair is one of only few segments to be written in these predawn hours, and though of the three it aspires to most thoroughly dissect Roubaud's project, far more has continued to emerge of self-reflection. Such is the true nature of Roubaud's creation. So often described as his Proustian work, it shares very little with it, except in its honest analysis of the concurrence and presentness of memory, and moreso, externally, in its education of the reader in mastering, and being honest with the mechanics of memory, making the reader a giant, "perched on its giddy summit... looked down beneath... as though from a height, which was (their) own height, of many leagues, at the long series of the years." Whether by conscious intent or not, the other shared characteristic with Proust, wrought in this case by Roubaud's tactic of writing continuously, austerely and singularly, without iteration, against the "Flaubertian toil upon the sentences," not editing, is the shared superabundance of commas.*

There is a presentness, not of the bespoke mold of the individual life, in mediated concurrence. A similar species to concurrence with the diffused personal constellation, this is a stepping into the physical space that has been prepared by a representation calibrated for all. A traveler arriving for the first time in Paris does not fully register, does not sense the discovery of a place in such a mediated prerecollection until they have become concurrent with that representation. In the mediated concurrence with a place, there is even a small geographic area, a refined vantage, one must occupy to lock into the discovery   → Δ 2. The only escape is to avoid that prerecollection. Best of luck. Yes, one can go to Paris and experience unexpected pleasures, but they cannot be experienced in that Paris, in that moment, but in the Paris concurrent with the mold constructed within, from elsewhere. Consequently, one instead experiences Paris more truly later, by surprise, in a place like Lawrence, Kansas. The mediated concurrence is not relegated to the spatial. This text you are reading, as a whole, occurs within the presentness of Roubaud's project, where Roubaud's opus exists for me, much like his suspicion of "pictions," as a found representation of a thought I believe I've had about the nature of memory. However layered and fluid Roubaud's text, it exists in that homogenous frozen "piction" state that leads efforts or experiences in its wake to be mere recapitulations of its silhouette, like Roubaud's description of photographs of his childhood home, rather than the recollection of the moment →Δ 1.

That I would not have any awareness of my future, would not on my first encounters grant icons of my future the significance I later accord upon them, is not odd, it is in fact necessary, because those things that in silent diligence grow to be the canyon walls of the life mold are not noteworthy. They become noteworthy only in the happenstance constellation of our duration with them. Those things which are immediately remarkable—a film, a place, a face in the crowd—are such because their seeds had been sown themselves far earlier as innocuous tendencies and landmarks of personal development that came to shape that perfectly matched mnemonic receptacle, that prerecollection, in the present. The discovered object is not remarkable in itself, but in the way it fits into or completes the latent constellation. The constellation of past experiences that fabricate that receptacle must be irretrievable, metamorphosed into the material of the mold, for the encounter with this object, this very rare concurrence with the present, to be such, rather than an act of recognition. It must have the aura of *discovery to become embedded indelibly in that present, otherwise the search begins for what precipitated its appropriateness in the past, and its corpus in the present is thus relocated.*

The experience at the moment, the property that characterizes this inscription, is wind. As quickly as it is acknowledged, the wind is gone, difficult to recall. I can write, "the wind," but it is not an image, it is only physical in its indexes, autumn leaves clattering in a tree, prayer flags lapping, long hair Gorgonized, or far from this landlocked house, waves lapping or crashing onto a still beach, the index of a distant aeolian system like dead starlight always in transit, eclipsed on this vector by an empty shingle. I recall coming to Kansas City for the first time in 2009, the airport desolate in a grassland, characterized only by incessant wind. And I recall later, just after writing about Pedernales Falls, coming to Kansas City again in 2012 to plan a move from Eugene to Lawrence, being greeted by that wind and asking the person at the rental car lot if it was windy like this all the time and he said yes pretty much it is. And distinct from all of that, driving from Los Angeles to Richmond in the summer of 2000, stopping for a night outside of Manhattan, Kansas to camp at a reservoir where my parents had camped when they drove across the country in their Camaro in the summer of 1970. Rainless wind all night beat down my dome-tent such that it pressed against me lying on the floor. And certainly, absolutely, within a couple of hours the following day I would have driven by Lawrence on Interstate 70 and not noticed it, because why would I take notice of something lingering in my future, something that, in its state today, windy, sunny, mid 50°s, the day after hundreds of people were murdered in terrorist attacks on Paris, did not even exist yet. And oddly, though I am well aware of my history in Kansas, I'm not certain it would seem at all interconnected without the wind, an arbitrary property, so easy for even the least observant to seize upon, yet, and at to my current awareness, that's all I am present with of the past, and some days it's not all that windy, and it's too quiet.

My trip to Pedernales Falls was like a concurrence with a memory of the future. It was an experience from its memory, the orgy of details ascending and spreading and blooming all over from a germ of an inkling. The fact that I was there very late in my tenure as a fetus

probably bears little on the diffused sense of recognition I had emerging into the strangely small clearing that this bulge of the river hollowed. In fact, had I any senses at the time, the memory would more likely be of something forgotten. Δ *Where the experience is typically the point, and the memory is the expanding diffused territory, here the experience exists at the broadened end of the memory expanding out from the point of its immaculate origin.* The singularity in question here was a trip my family took over the Bicentennial weekend to Pedernales Falls from College Station, Texas thirty-eight days before I was born. My mother, obviously incredibly pregnant, spent the afternoon sliding down the water-smoothed rocks with my father and sister and a family called the Simonets, whom I have actually met and have of course forgotten. My mother was allegedly the subject of some hand-wringing from the older ladies among the revelers. She paid no mind and had a great time with me in her nestled in the dark. Two yellowed and unconvincing photos exist from that day. These two photos create the sensory construct of this memory when conjoined with family lore and the atmosphere of the national holiday. The nineteen-seventies seem to have been a bad time for hobby photography. Pictures always seem to have been captured in motion Δ *such that they all have an unresolved vagueness, though perhaps more reflective of the moment's transience than the thousands of crisp, well-balanced images each of us now have sequestered from reality in our phones* and I wonder how quickly those prints grew icteric from exposure, or if those particular photos arrived from a drive-up fotomat in a College Station parking lot already shivering away from the moment of their birth with a gamy case of jaundice. But it was my Δ *truly* simultaneous presence and absence at Pedernales Falls that causes the memory to start at zero and be built over time, as if my emerging from the trees this past Sunday (July 4, 1976 was a Sunday) was not into a place that had always been there but had been sculpted and tuned by my musings of thirty-five years approaching it. Thus, the sensations of dusk sun on the rock and still pools, the sound of my shoes in loose river stone and of white water in carved sluices, the cooler air, the bugs alighting on my face, of the basin's relative scale in the way that it both cradled and constantly receded from my body, of dry seed pods quaking like rattles from bundles of tall dry stems, of gravity tugging at me as my worn soles slid down polished rock steps, the remaining sun's rays sneaking as coronas about foliage atop the bluff seemed more real than real life, though in its more insistent and symphonic immersion, felt also less real, more like a terrain snuck from the tangible sand of memory. I know that I felt this sensation, this diffusion that I feel more and more, acutely on the falls. Yet, when I leapt back up the rocks into the trees, the dislocation of the experience from the real structure of my life began quickly to devolve into how I might describe it, what words might characterize something, a process that began just before I was born, that had now culminated, had ceased, had died peacefully, in order to slow the taper of that entire lifetime and its oddly ultimate horizontal precipice. But in mining and processing the memory, as Roubaud indicates in "The Loop," which I am now reading, which after days of dwelling emotionally on the experience prompted me to take out my pad after reading his assertion that the future too is a form of memory, writing the memory, giving it form, kills it. Or, more precisely, "I destroy (the image) in the sense that, becoming weaker and paler, it doesn't so much disappear as become something I can no longer evoke, no longer revisit except as a second-order memory, the memory of my remembering it, and of all the moments in which I insistently contemplated it during the time spent on its description, under the effect of the words and thoughts that this description gives rise to." I occupy the space now, by analogy, after the stiffness of senility's tissue has allowed the trace of the initial experience through memory to at last escape the physics of the world, or in this case, to a point prior to that singular origin of my mother sliding down the rock, prior to the coalescence of my being. But I don't think it is quite so inversely proportional

diagrammatically. As I continue to live, think, and recall the entire wedge of the future memory and its satisfaction will now, as a flattened, weakened and empaled, package, taper towards my death as a typical memory. Though in its ascent I did not consider the future memory more regularly than a past memory surfaces in my mind, I am led to consider, in the constant flickering, what other possibilities for future memories are shuffled into my mind, or whether it is a once in a lifetime sensation.

Δ 1   I don't care much for snapshots taken by other people, they never train on what I am interested in seeing, they have no significance to me. I want the freedom to see something that could only be seen in the place, I want the space of the frame chewed and broken, and I want to do it myself.

Δ 2   *An artist, Corinne Vionnet, produced a series of layered images composed of photographs taken by travelers of various landmarks like the Eiffel Tower, the Taj Mahal, the Ka'aba, all within a shiver distance of the same perspective. Visually, remarkably similar to the photograph taken by Alix Roubaud, "Fifteen Minutes at Night to a Respiratory Rhythm," considered by her husband Jacques Roubaud less for its subject matter of cypress trees than its indexicality of his late wife's breathing, "a photograph of her breath," these photos are also concerned with the effect of subjectivity over duration, though very different in ethos, Vionnet's the mediated memory, Mme Roubaud's the fleeting contingency of the singular.*

When I walk into the Marriott Marquis, in these more recent days of distraction, I am guided by habit, the key moments at which I know I have to turn, to ascend, to choose, are triangulated by visual cues, which tend to be the only things I see, I hardly look up anymore into the enormous hollow volume, I rarely notice the elevators with their carnivalesque rows of lights, a trademark of early John Portman, I merely fix on what is necessary to pilot my route, without wonder or scrutiny. I do many things this way, I often read this way because the words fall apart, they are so familiar, the grammar so rote that I read every few words glossing over the connective tissue whose character I either extrapolate or ignore because it is useless, it is a vehicle for travel between points. If the nature of space is such that I color the intermediate tissue myself, why should I not begin without that tissue, requiring fresh wonder for every interaction.

One theory of cognitive mapping takes into account our shared expectations and prior engagements with situations and spaces throughout our lives in order to explain how we frame the spaces we encounter in a particular setting around those in the same setting that we did not encounter, whether forbidden, redundant, or inconsequential. Our cognitive map of a cafe is constructed around the fragment we engage, the dining area and the storefront, and against the space we did not engage, the kitchen, even though we know it is behind the blank wall opposite the storefront. Like the blank page upon which the murder is committed in "Le Voyeur," or the reflection of television glow on the ceiling in every upper room of every convalescent home is completed by my unconscious grandfather who is not visible, we construct our environment from fragments, we live in an incomplete, individually perceived, unfinished environment.

The ruin is not in the truth of decay, or the false longing of the anachronous soul, but is dependent upon loss, for it is only in the evacuation of the face, the touch, the personality, the culture, and the context that we truly invest our whole being.   Δ *How lovely to think of the loss of Greek polychrome and how, through Roman misappropriation, it continues to affect our ideals of beauty.*   Human-present endeavors are consumed with discorporated distraction for the other. The ruin is the freedom from this, it need not be the decayed structure, "sunlight on a broken column," or even possessed of decay in any capacity, it must merely be emptied of its potential to recall life.

I am sitting under a table-lamp in the cavernous lobby of the Marriott Marquis again because it has grown so familiar to me. Although I have finalized a preferred route into and through its bowels, it still perplexes me. One theory on the way individuals remember and order space in their minds proposes a cognitive map that is not Euclidean, not physical, but a collection of images, icons, frames, and passages tethered by the experiences undergone to apprehend them. There are no right turns or left turns or paces or elapsed times, there is a fluid catalog in the mind that is spatial in an instantaneous, manifold way that space can never occur. Writing this is the elision of potential space and difference for immediacy and emptiness.

I write backwards from the zenith, where fragments, tossed out from a single point, arc at their most scattered, having only to wait for the pull of gravity to bind them together again. I write back toward that singularity in the project, the only point thus far where there has been a project, I seek to write backward through archival time, while necessarily moving forward through real time to a point, to a mirrored conclusion, an inversion of the understanding and naivety that was the decision to begin this work, because all things seek ruin.

On these bound blue lines, with such clear definitions, on this stack of cards I will write, in words, what could not be writ in the haphazard lines and values of the draughtsman's pencil, and not over the months that eclipse into earlier darkness, when I arrive home to a desk in darkness to cough out shapes. I want to see architecture itself, as a practice, ruined, *Δ At the moment, three volumes of Roubaud's project are available in English, the titular "The Great Fire of London", "The Loop", and "Mathematics:". The final of the three has least to do with memory, more to do with the sensibility of the project, and of my local project, in that it considers the impact of parallel practice on the project of writing, in Roubaud's case, mathematics, in mine, architecture* I want its representations to slide onto the paper in such a way as to belie their infancy. I want it immediately ancient, with me erased, so that the ruinous history given to people all at once could be immediately claimed by them, broken down, individuated, owned by anybody but me. I want this nightly sacrifice of my time, my sleepless hours, my self-worth to be pushed toward so much nothing that I could not be blamed for it.

What Next?:
The Future of the Humanities

STEPHANIE JANE JONES

The pleasure of difficulty has always been the driving force behind Christine Brooke-Rose's fiction. Whether this comes in the form of the dislocation and dissociation of the reader as in *Out* (1964), *Such* (1966) and *Amalgamemnon* (1984), code-switching between languages as in *Between* (1968) or with impressive typographical gymnastics as demonstrated in *Thru* (1975) and *Next* (1998), Brooke-Rose demands that the reader do more than simply sit and receive a fully formed narrative. The 'difficulties' that Brooke-Rose presents for the reader encapsulate that which she regards to be the true pleasure of reading: the process of working out the puzzle is the most enjoyable part. For Brooke-Rose, this enjoyment of difficulty extends to learning, and education in a broader sense. However, what happens when the pleasure of the difficulty diminishes and is replaced by easily accessible visual and digital forms? Within her fiction, Brooke-Rose expresses a growing concern for the future of literature and the competency of the contemporary readership more generally. While Brooke-Rose's earlier experimentalism plays with complex structures, her later work expresses an anxiety that society is losing touch with humanity and the "fundamentals" that are so often expressed in literature. This is seen only too clearly in the anxiety that permeates the collection of novels described by Brooke-Rose as the "Intercom Quartet".

This niggle of anxiety begins in *Amalgamemnon* with Mira Enketi mourning her own position as a redundant classics professor: "as redundant as you after queue" (5); it increases through the "alien" invasion in *Xorandor* and the silencing of the "eternal commentary" (27) in *Verbivore*, before culminating in *Textermination* with the destruction of the San Francisco Hilton Hotel, burying classic literary characters under the rubble. With these novels, Brooke-Rose engages with the social fear that the general readership is becoming less capable, their attention becoming increasingly distracted by technology and the instant gratification that digital and visual media can deliver. She also gestures towards the contemporary debate of the survival of literature in the digital era and specifically, literary characters as defined, comprehensive entities. Jeremy Green has encapsulated this debate by stating that

> Any power to shape the larger culture is now or soon
> will be greatly restricted as the larger culture turns
> increasingly towards electronic media [...] For the
> pessimist, the novel seems doomed to enjoy no more
> than a coterie following, its bygone authority dissipated
> or taken over by electronic cultural forms (45-46).

While the "Intercom Quartet" confronts these issues head-on, emphasising their immediacy, her tenth experimental novel *Next* outlines the effects of this diminished, culturally unmotivated readership after the turn towards technology. *Next*, along with Brooke-Rose's other later novels, has received even less critical attention than her earlier work. However, it is clear that it remains concerned with the same issues of redundancy, replacement and automation that permeate the "Intercom Quartet".

While *Next* displays all of the inherent traits that have become recognisable as defining Brooke-Rose's fiction (the use of the "scientific present tense" (*Rhetoric of the Unreal*, 140), language puns, the juxtaposition of numerous narrative voices) it can be primarily described as a murder mystery novel.* Each of the twenty-six characters that appear in the novel is named after each of the letters on a standard English "QWERTY" keyboard. The ten main characters that the novel follows have names that begin with letters from the top line of the keyboard: "QWERTYUIOP". The reader's knowledge of this constraint immediately reveals Brooke-Rose's preoccupation with language in the novel and indeed, it is not a hidden constraint; rather, it is disclosed in the blurb that appears on the back cover of the book. However, within the body of the novel lies a further constraint—a lipogram: the omission of the verb "to have". This constraint is related directly to the plot of the novel and to its main characters who are all homeless people living on the streets of London. The omission of the verb "to have" illustrates the relationship that these characters have to material belongings, emphasising that they have nothing. Not only are these people entirely devoid of possessions, but as well as being "without", they have been "dispossessed" by the state and society. Indeed, early on in the novel, the homeless are referred to as "Drop-outs" (9) implying their removal or omission from society. Further emphasis is added to this situation when the author plays upon the difference between the words "in" and "out", manipulating terms such as the "Drop-In Centre", which instead appears as "Drop-Out Centre" (9). This subtle linguistic replacement asserts that these homeless characters do not exist as part of the working societal machine of London but rather, they live outside of society and its bounds, haunting the city like ghostly spectres, visible only to each other.

Brooke-Rose uses the lipogram as a constraint to great effect in her earlier novel *Between* where the omission of the verb "to be" reflects the experience of the female translator protagonist, whose existence is in continual flux; she is continually between countries, between relationships and between languages. As in *Between*, the lipogram is hidden in *Next* and without a very keen grammatical eye, or an

---

* The "scientific present tense" is referred to by Brooke-Rose in *Rhetoric of the Unreal* to describe the sustained use of the speakerless present tense when used in critical writing or scientific law. She describes the term as having originated from film where a "quasi-neutral camera" is used in order to be as objective as possible in its depiction of a story or event.

explanation from the author, it is unlikely that the reader would even notice this experiment. The ease with which this lipogram goes unnoticed reflects the way in which society ignores the homeless of London. Brooke-Rose depicts the homeless as a societal lipogram: human beings that have been omitted from society, skimmed over, hidden or ignored. Considering Brooke-Rose's earlier examples (with the exception of *Out*'s race reversal metaphor), it perhaps seems strange that she should take such a pertinent, emotional societal issue for the narrative content of her novel. Nevertheless, it seems apt (albeit a little pessimistic) to use homelessness as a metaphor for the state of the humanities in academia and education in a more general sense, as the onus placed upon the ability to be technologically capable seems to have overpowered knowledge of the arts and philosophy in contemporary society. With this novel, Brooke-Rose positions the humanities and humanity itself as being omitted from the curriculum of contemporary life. While this metaphor is conveyed on a reasonably subtle level by the narrative focus upon the homeless, it is explored in much closer detail with the individual characters of the text.

Most of the main characters have a background in some sort of cultural pursuit, history or the arts: Ulysses is a former English teacher who spent his earlier life travelling around Africa, experiencing different cultures; Pavlova is a former ballet dancer; Oliver is Eton and Oxford educated and Elsie has some previous experience in teaching: a skill that she manages to trade for food. This collection of homeless redundant and former artistic types in *Next* transforms Mira Enketi's fears in *Amalgamemnon* into a reality. The redundancy of culture and artistic skills and their replacement with capabilities in unscrupulous digital media is exactly what Mira fears for her own future:

> Who will want to read at night some utterly other discourse that will shimmer out of a minicircus of light upon a page of say Agamemnon [...] The new generation will supertouchtype programmes and games all to be superdevised by an elite of supertechnicians [...](5-6).

However, the characters in *Next* have no future to fear, instead, they are doomed to live their fears in the present.

Almost all of the homeless characters try to escape their fate by applying for a job at the unscrupulous technology company "Cuter Computers". Elsie explains the hardships of being a female homeless, and hopes to change her status within society by gaining employment at this firm. She explains that she has spent her "last few pounds on painkillers and sannies no tampax for me I bleed too bleeding much" (68). She longs for a "little flat somewhere, a room a kitchenette a bath a loo of one's own" (68), playing on Virginia Woolf's demands in *A Room of One's Own* (1929). By punning on Woolf's polemic, Brooke-Rose draws some parity between the essentiality of a writing room for a middle-class woman and a lavatory for a homeless woman in an effort to draw a comparison between the priorities of women from different means. Elsie's needs seem so much more immediate and basic in comparison. However, her role in educating the illiterate Portuguese immigrant Lin (Adelina) reminds the reader that the education of the woman in society is just as much a priority as her basic human rights. Lin is married to Xavier who is unable to read or write English and is able to speak very little. He is not supportive of Lin's education and resents Elsie for visiting the house and teaching Lin how to read and write, especially when she repays Elise with the offer of food: "Now she's insisting on me staying to share the curry and Xavier at once transmits a not-enough-to-go-round scowl" (43). Elsie reluctantly leaves the house and returns to the streets where eventually she meets her fate. It is reported that she has been murdered, and possibly raped by an unknown assailant (82). The removal of Elsie from the narrative is significant as it removes the character "E" from the text. This can be regarded as yet another pun by Brooke-Rose: a play on Georges Perec's idea of his own commercially successful lipogram: the omission of the letter "e" in his novel *La Disparition* (1968). Brooke-Rose was both aware of Perec's novel, as well as being an admirer of his work, and her novel *Between* had been compared to *La Disparition* as both were published within six months of each other, and both used lipograms for technical effect. Both *Next* and *La Disparition* are murder mystery novels, and there is a sense that Brooke-Rose's removal of "E" from her text is an acknowledgement of the omitted "character" from Perec's earlier work. In *La Disparition*, the protagonist Anton Vowl is missing from the text and the other characters (along with the reader) embark on a quest to find him by reading his papers and attempting to piece together his whereabouts. Similarly, after Elsie's murder and her consequent removal from the text, the reader and some of the other characters are anxious to find out who is responsible for the crime by retracing her last movements, but to no avail.

Elsie's last moments are omitted from the text, and the reader is left to retrace her steps around London in search of any clues. While narrating her way around the streets, Elsie often slips into reciting the alphabet, finding various human atrocities to assign to each letter: "A for Apartheid, I for Indian Reservations [...] J for Jihad K for Khmer Rouge [...]"(69). By removing her from the text, Brooke-Rose removes all of the qualities that she and her "E character" stand for, including "education" and "equality". In her narrations of these atrocities, she often becomes obstructed by the letter "H" even though "there's usually more than one horror for each letter" (3): "H for what? Funny how H always blocks" (35). Elsie's inability to find words beginning with "H" can be regarded as a linguistic depiction of her inability "to have" and to find "humanity" within society. "H Blocks" also reminds the reader of HM Prison Maze in Northern Ireland, located outside County Down, used throughout the 1970s until the early 2000s to detain political prisoners during the Troubles. In an article written about the impending closure of the prison in 2000, Ted Oliver explains that the prison had been given the nickname "the university of terror" due to its ability to transform amateur terrorists into professionals who became well-versed in bomb making and who could withstand even the most rigorous interrogation. The protests that the prisoners made to their detainment were extreme, including the refusal to wear prison uniforms, smashing furniture, and hunger strikes. As a result, the H-blocks have become a notorious yet significant part of

British and Irish history. Brooke-Rose's engagement with this political context and indeed, all of the other human atrocities of which Elsie makes note, she confronts the dichotomies that are inherent within our society: life/death, existence/survival, freedom/restriction. By confronting these oppositions, the author gestures towards dispossession on a larger scale, emphasising the futility of human actions, forcing the reader to recognise the human race's preoccupation with its own destruction.

Although Brooke-Rose's earlier fiction can and has been criticised for being too concerned with aestheticism and the superficiality of language games (Cunningham, 1975; Ackroyd, 1975), it is clear that her later work engages more directly with contemporary societal concerns. With *Next*, Brooke-Rose confronts the issues of homelessness and dispossession head-on, asserting that the inevitability of the destruction of humanity is a fate that has been sealed by our own actions: the closer we get to digital autonomy, the further away we drift from our own humanity. For Brooke-Rose, "humanity" is the missing character in the language of this "brave new world".

Works Cited

Brooke-Rose, Christine, *A Rhetoric of the Unreal* (London: Cambridge University Press, 1981)

----------, *Amalgamemnon* (Manchester: Carcanet Publishing, 1984)

----------, *Verbivore* (Manchester: Carcanet, 1991)

----------, *Next* (Manchester: Carcanet, 1998)

Green, Jeremy, *Late Postmodernism: American Fiction at the Millennium* (Hampshire: Palgrave MacMillian, 2005)

Oliver, Ted, "H-Block To Slam Door on Grim History", *Telegraph* (23/07/2000). Accessed online:

http://www.telegraph.co.uk/news/uknews/1349997/H-blocks-to-slam-door-on-a-grim-history.htmlt

Pilgrim of the Absolute:
An Interview with Alexander Theroux

THOMAS FILBIN

Alexander Theroux, novelist, poet, and essayist, is a man deliberately out of sync with his times. His work is both postmodernist and neo-classical, and he weaves both sensibilities into his writing. His mentality is that of a Renaissance man, while he tweaks and insults the mundane thoughtlessness of modern life far too hung up on appearance and dogma. It is no coincidence that "Thoreau" and "Theroux" play on one another. He is a man who marches to the beat of his own drummer.

His most recent novel *Laura Warholic, or The Sexual Intellectual* and his *Collected Poems* have been published by Fantagraphics Books. He answered some questions recently by e-mail from his home on Cape Cod, Massachusetts.

TF: Did you write at a very early age?

AT: On rainy days when we were tots we diddled and doodled with pencils and crayons. As preadolescents, our deeply committed, proud, and engaging father who had a distinct historical bent, as well as an abiding love of old Boston, Concord, Lexington, and environs, on Sunday afternoons would dutifully take his young boys on local treks and to various historic places—"take-ins" he called them—places like the Old North Church, "Old Ironsides," the Agassiz Museum, Walden Pond, Concord Bridge, Jack gardner's Palace, the whaling museum in New Bedford, the House of the Seven Gables, etc.). When we returned my parents encouraged us to write small essays in our composition books on what we had remembered and experienced. Our folks also read to us on most nights at bedtime, and we actually grew up thrilling to names like James Fenimore Cooper, Edgar Allan Poe, Robert Louis Stevenson, Charles Dickens, Washington Irving. "Great Authors"—peopling my dreams—were then, as now my only heroes.

I was also deeply influenced by radio programs back in the 1940s and early radio drama (*Mr. Keen, Tracer of Lost Persons, Sky King, The Lone Ranger, Lights Out, Cavalcade of America*, etc.) as well as early Disney movies (*Pinocchio, Cinderella, Dumbo*). I recall with nostalgia watching on television an early sci-fi film called *The Phantom Empire* starring Gene Autry that for its imaginative narrative, and odd music plunked me full-scale into the weird world of fiction and made me pine for and dream of writing stories.

TF: Coover, Barth, and Pynchon published in the 1960s; did they influence you with a new way of writing (not conventional realism), or was the metafictional impulse something that was gestating in you on its own?

AT: Those three meant nothing to me. My eye was focused both earlier and later on denser, classic, more magnetic writers. I was fascinated even in high school with Shakespeare, the Jacobean playwrights, the novels of Dickens, Juvenal, *The Aeneid*, Laurence Sterne's *Tristram Shandy* (speaking of metafiction!), Alexander Pope. Homer. I can still fondly recall many details from childhood favorites of mine, *School Days in Disneyville* (1939), *Winnie the Pooh, Make Way for Ducklings, The Five Chinese Brothers*, Dr. Seuss's *The 500 hats of Bartholomew Cubbins, Epaminondas, So Dear to My Heart, Sonny Elephant*, etc.

TF: Did your experiences in religious life carry over to your writing later?

AT: The church taught me about the mystery of wandering, what Gabriel Marcel called "*homo viator*", man the wayfarer, man the pilgrim, man in transit, man on a journey through this valley of tears. My dreams of writing were never unconnected with the metaphysical aspects that asked who we are and why and where we are all going, questions of being and becoming, of faith and disbelief. I have been saturated since I was a boy in the Christian mystery and miracle. I can honestly say I am literally astonished when meeting thinkers whose questions and answers to the universe are different. In this regard, Christopher Hitchens, whom I knew in passing—we won Lannan Grants together in 1991—could have come from another planet.

TF: Some critics have called your work misogynistic. The easy question would be: "Do you deny that this is so?" A harder question is: "Even though you disagree, do you see why they feel this way?

AT: Women and cars (car trouble at the side of the road) alone have made me weep in life! Seriously, love, the conflicts of love, jealousy, abandonment and loss of love and all its variants, provide the most intriguing plots in fiction. I have written as satirically about men as I have of women. Dr. Crucifer, a character in my novel, *Darconville's Cat* (1982), was an articulate and mad, rant-oriented misogynist, however, and someone whom I had so much fun writing about, making him if I may say so indelibly drawn, that he gave serious ammunition, I suspect, to a good many readers who committing the "intentional fallacy" blithely chose to attribute his particular follies to me. I must say I do find women remarkably different than men, lovelier, at times more comical, warmer, certainly strung with opposite wires.

TF: Do you think of yourself more as a poet or a novelist, or are they two sides of the same coin?

AT: I cannot imagine a good writer not being able to write well in any genre, essays, plays, novels, poetry. Still, Herman Melville wasn't a good poet, Hardy was. So was Poe. Hemingway wasn't, neither was Malcolm Lowry, nor Thomas Pynchon, for that matter. It depends on your concentration, one's needs. Henry James yearned to be a playwright but failed. Did he ever write any poetry? I don't believe so. Oscar Wilde wrote a good novel and much good poetry and splendid plays. Life is brief. We are forced to choose our tournaments. I think energy accounts for a lot in the matter. Jonathan Swift was a .400 hitter.

TF: Will canonical works like *War and Peace* just disappear because people are too busy or too engaged in the digital world and don't hold literary traditions as important as they once were?

AT: Tragically, or it seems to me, young people nowadays with their twittering and facebooking fascinations do not seem to need, to want, to love, or to choose books like *War and Peace*. It is not even in the conversation, is it? It is the Pilgrim of the Absolute who is a seeker. Why else are we here? I explained to my students that the sole and singular purpose of living was to find out the *meaning* of it. Were not Prince Andre and Pierre and Natasha classic examples of such seekers? We seem to lack the *gravitas* of that need nowadays, or possibly I am just too old to see it in play. We all of us need to be wayfarers to find the need to read—and to be constructively disturbed by!—books like *Crime and Punishment, The Brothers Karamazov, War and Peace.* One should never be the same after reading such books. It is a holy search—to be a quester. J. Alfred Prufrock for all of his faults was at least *asking* meaningful questions; I would warn my students who when reading T.S. Eliot's poem would often cheaply find a need to mock Prufrock as a textbook neurotic, but in his way he was brave. We all of us live in parlous times, indeed. The church with its many pedophile scandals, hideous salacities, cover-ups, and corruptions seems in ways no longer a help, a church in which vocations are way down and the banalities of secularism prevail. There is a kind of Cartesian dislocation, a loss of a sense of place, that we now suffer—in a sense we can no longer find ourselves (if indeed we are looking) on the Great Chain of Being. In an interview on the occasion of his Jefferson Lecture in 1989 ('The Fateful Rift: The San Andreas Fault in the Modern Mind') Walker

Percy spoke of modern man as being "*deranged*, the literal sense of that term most appropriate to the Cartesian dislocation of the intellect that has hastened our displacement from a sense of being in the world," according to Marion Montgomery in *Walker Percy and the Christian Scandal*. What, Percy wanted to know, were the options for characters populating this deranged world in which the church is no longer regnant, in fact a literal scandal in so many places. I fear that far too many people look around and see no derangement at all. Pathetic.

TF: In the same vein: do you see appreciation for words and language receding in the shorthand of today's texting, compression of communications, and slang? Are people and language becoming estranged?

AT: We live in an age of supreme scruple. For all the so-called "communications" I see a fund of electronic equipment and lots of palaver and gabbling and email and talk shows and texting, if that is the correct word. I get the impression all of it consists of monologues and not dialogues.

TF: Are you a writer ahead of your time or behind it?

AT: Way behind the times. I don't believe that I have very many readers as a result. I have never tailored my work for big sales nor written with a view to the screen. I am in the old George Eliot-mode, the old novel form, long chapters. It is a precarious business to be a writer of books. My book sales are and have always been meager and in fact truly embarrassing. I have published to date ten books—fiction, non-fiction, and poetry. I have six more completed manuscripts in boxes ready to be published. Not one of the eighty-eight essays that I have written and that have over the years been printed in magazines have been published in book form. I have no agent. My advances are small, almost derisive. Our little family is food-card poor.

On Jeff Bursey's Verbatim: A Novel

G.N. FORESTER

Content follows form. What is the offspring of a union between the format of parliamentary papers and a wickedly acute eye for exposing the foibles of both the political system, its practitioners, its adherents, its supplicants, and its auxiliaries? Jeff Bursey's debut *Verbatim: A Novel.* Fiction revealed as faction? Or fact overhauled as fiction? Bursey employs a touch of Swiftian genius which presents satire as that plausible thin line between the casuistry of the one extreme collapsing to the sophistry of its polar opposite, irrespective of whichever side of the political fence the reader might prefer to occupy. That is the relentless, elegant beauty of this entirely fictional exposé concerning events during the 1990s in a contemporary Atlantic Canadian Province, naturally unnamed.

To place the structure (and exquisite attention to detail entailed in the form) of Bursey's work in context requires an historical detour. Hansard (the Official Report) is the edited verbatim report of parliamentary proceedings (debates is the most oft quoted label: as Bursey ably demonstrates, a euphemism for what typically degenerates to squabbles in the sandbox, with appropriate tactics for upsetting and exploiting the established 'rules') for the UK and member Commonwealth countries and former UK colonies. It evolved from the lack of public availability (or conversely protection of Parliamentary privilege) of the debates in the UK Parliament in the late eighteenth century, although tabled actions were made public. In order to thwart the law, newspapers published scantily disguised articles describing the undisclosed sessions. One such vociferous critic, William Cobbett, wrote an article for which he was later sentenced to fines and imprisonment. The article was published by Thomas Hansard and when Cobbett encountered hard times, his collection of written recordings passed to Hansard in 1812, transitioning from *Cobbett's Parliamentary Debates* to *Hansard Parliamentary Debates* and finally *Hansard*. Ironically, neither Cobbett nor Hansard were present during sessions to take notes, instead editions were cobbled together from newspapers. Half a century after the issuance of the first edition bearing Hansard's name, the press received a grant to hire reporters to record the Parliamentary proceedings, but complaints as to the veracity of accounts were frequent. In 1893 a special committee created Hansard terms of reference, such that in effect the official Hansard transcripts have *never* been verbatim accounts of debates, but actively massaged; redundancies, repetitions, unanswered interjections, and grammatical or minor factual inaccuracies (but since the document is "factual", a Parliamentary Member making an inaccurate statement is required to present in writing an accurate statement to amend the Parliamentary Library copy of Hansard) being deleted, although nothing of material importance is supposed to be omitted. In 1909, staff were hired by Parliament to record sessions, and thereafter Hansard was published under the auspices of the Houses.

Elsewhere, such as in Canada, newspapers spearheaded the initiative for freedom of the press, publishing the debates, and the UK convention was adopted, although not all aspects, and not by all provinces simultaneously (as recently as 1981 did one province have no official recording). The interjections of Canadian Parliamentary Members are signified by "Some hon. Members: Oh, oh!", employed to grim and humorous effect by Bursey, along with "Some Hon. Members: Hear, hear!", and the neat twist of "inaudible" (the conventional term is "interruption", covering a multitude of sins considered to reflect badly on the sobriety invested in the institution of Parliament) when indiscretions are rubbed out by his Hansard Editors, generally viewing transcribers with long-sufferance and each other with disdain and the new Hansard

Director, hired to improve Hansard and the department, with antipathy and suspicion.

The book thus comprises the format of 'verbatim' debates recorded by staff employed to ensure Parliamentarians are presented in a not-unflattering light, while still upholding the grand traditions of political debate (and Bursey deftly shows these to be the buffoonery that characterise the antics of a two-party system whose ideologies coincide: namely, how to manipulate opinion by insinuation and casting aspersion, and to exploit pressing social and economic issues for the purposes of either bellicose obfuscation or personal gain) and democracy (the choice between a highway robber on one side and a pirate on the other?). Mere pages after the book opens in the two columned Hansard style indicating the speaker, the Speaker, and the Hon. Members, a short series of emails (differentiated by font as well as caption) between the Clerk and the Speaker follow, setting the stage for the unfortunate stooge played by the soon-to-be-appointed Hansard Director, but also clearly displaying their personalities and happily ruthless capacity to extract full advantage from any given situation. Thereafter the characters are introduced as would be the cast of a play, with names and constituencies and political affiliation, at the opening the Fourth Session, epigraphed with the delightfully insightful quotation from the preface of the sixth edition of *Beauchesne's Parliamentary Rules and Forms*, published by Arthur Beauchesne, Clerk of the Canadian House of Commons 1925-1949: "The broadcasting of the proceedings of the House and the change in emphasis on the question period have given to the public a new and sometimes unflattering as well as distorted impression of political debate." Image management consultants could probably take lessons.

Not in the first roll call and conspicuous by absence are any Independent Members bar one, continually prevented from contributing to debate; for non-Canadian readers this appears a curious aberration, until later in the proceedings, when the dual-party stranglehold over the House is broken, and the legislatively entrenched basis for smothering speech is revealed.

Thus the reader is effectively presented, and at times accompanied by the changing audiences in the gallery, with a "live" Parliamentary performance of some sixty-eight individuals, all who are made equal, except that some are more equal than others, and some will disappear to be replaced at the whim of voters, as well as the supporting cast of technicians, department heads (Library, Finance etc), transcribers (absent-but-present by virtue of transcripts being created), the two warring Editors, and the Hansard Director, whose lines are always relayed via emails, but whose personalities are immediately evident. To Bursey's credit, these are stereotypes avoiding cliché, in particular the well-meaning Hansard Director is saved from bourgeois heroism by a distinctly victim-like tone entering late in the game, suggesting, if not proving, that when playing with politicians and their bureaucratic groupies, blatant goodwill and pursuit of a principled stand is a successful strategy for being made the patsy when the behavioural change program backfires—if corruption festers at the summit of the food-chain, it infects all the way down.

The material spans the gamut of politically sensitive topics in a period of depression and economic difficulty, encompassing but not limited to the behaviour of Big Business in the persona of resource extraction companies, management of the health care system, initiatives to improve (or destroy) education, amendments to various Bills which are, perhaps technically, not blocked by filibuster (and for one such incident is Canada notorious) but delayed in passage, detailing and derailing of public infrastructure projects, divides between ethnic groups, gender, rural and urban populations, and conflict over land use. The presentation, discussion, and resolution or failure thereof, of these topics in Parliament brilliantly identifies and characterises the various Party Members, but Bursey is careful never to cross the floor from or to either melancholy or melodrama, despite the attempts of Members to suck empathy from a situation to the best of their (dis)abilities.

The apparent conceit of the novel is that Hansard employees begin to mimic their political masters in the sense of contriving to ensure either inertia or change, ie not only does absolute power corrupt absolutely, but proximity to it does as well. But a focus purely on this aspect of the novel risks overlooking the carefulness with which Bursey juxtaposes the various claims, stakes, power shuffles and endgames of the political parties, as well as his ability to plausibly advocate from either corner of the floor, not to mention his pedantically detailed dates of Sessions, impetus for by-elections, inclusion of Question Period and Orders of the Day and introductions of Bills and basis for recess and points of order and recognition by the Chair. Moreover, textual discrepancies accumulate, adding to the twin realisations that while this is a work of fiction, even its 'truthful' rendering is false since the transcribers charged with producing transcripts of the proceedings are fallible in practice and flawed in ethics, if not approach, while the Editors are concerned with ensuring their idiosyncratic preferences (as an example, at one point "Some Hon. Members: Shame! Shame!" appears, just prior to the ostensible denouement and scapegoating of the Hansard Director).

Verbatim: A Novel must surely qualify as one of the most ueber-realistic postmodern satires yet penned and should hold interest not only for aficionados of the latter, but also those curious as to the nature of Parliamentary debates within an inherited, albeit modified, Westminster system; the quintessence of an Atlantic Canadian province; and a damning portrayal of the pettiness of human nature. Publishers Enfield & Wizenty are to be congratulated for the release of this inimitable novel.

Dialogic Imaginations:
Gabriel Josipovici's Recent Fictions

MONIKA FLUDERNIK

Gabriel Josipovici's predilection for the dialogue novel has often been commented on in reviews,[1] criticism,[2] and even by himself.[3] This emphasis on dialogue has to be placed side by side with other typical features of Josipovici's fiction and drama—his metafictional techniques, his modernist poetics, existentialist features and the thematics of exile and alienation.[4] Josipovici's work moreover displays a great many texts that foreground monologic utterances. Dialogue is therefore only *one* prominent distinctive feature of his oeuvre. Yet, in addition to some of the metafictional passages in the work, it is especially the nearly exclusive use of dialogue with very little narrative framing that has been perceived as the most striking formal aspect of his writing.

Gabriel Josipovici's two-novel volume *After & Making Mistakes: Two Novels* (2009) is another venture in the mode of the dialogue novel, yet I feel that in these texts he moves onto new ground in the use of this prominent narrative strategy. The two novels deploy a number of various techniques familiar from Josipovici's earlier writing. Most notable among these is the delineation of *verbal* communication as miscommunication or as a failure of mutual understanding (compare Fludernik 2000: 90-2). *After* and *Making Mistakes* also display a great amount of humour (a feature likewise commented on in Fludernik 2000: 94-8, 109-10), frequently linked to the routines of small talk (111-12).[5] However, these two novels go beyond such familiar strategies in approaching a representation of social gatherings that strongly reminded me of Woody Allen's films and their New York society setting,[6] though, in the case of *After*, the humour turns dark, develops a gruesome underside and becomes uncanny. In *Making Mistakes*, Josipovici infuses the dialogues with strong psychological significance and thereby achieves the unexpected effect of turning the seemingly ridiculous and inane into symptomatic verbal agency which is pregnant with diagnostic relevance. What Josipovici manages to do in the two texts under discussion is, therefore, to reboot the computer, using the same techniques for which his oeuvre has been known, but subtly refocusing the thematics in new directions. Whereas themes like loneliness, exile, existential anxiety and the absurdity of human life were the staple of earlier writings, here more specific situations (an accident, stalking, the break-up of a marriage) are being delineated, and an emphasis on man's alienation from society, especially on the constraints of heterosexual bonding, replaces the earlier interest in the single man alone in his room or in flight from any kind of human interaction.

For readers unfamiliar with the two texts, I would like to preface my discussion of each by a brief plot summary. Let me start with *After*.

The novel revolves around the relationship of Alan and Claude. Alan, now married to Sarah, quite unexpectedly runs into Claude at a party at his friend Sam Susskind's in London. The entire text is told from Alan's perspective to the extent that all scenes include Alan as a protagonist and we as readers follow his experiences, first at Sam's party (chapter I), then at a visit to his painter friend Simon, with his mother, his encounters in the pub, and his exchanges at home with his wife (chapter II). The novel is a typical instance of external focalization in the Genettian terminology. Chapter III has Alan on the phone with Claude; he meets Claude in chapter IV; in chapter V Alan visits Ronnie Chinn, finds himself in the doldrums; then Alan and Sarah are at a dinner party organized by Claude and her husband Byron (chapter VI). I dispense with the rest of the enumeration.

In the course of the novel, Claude continues to harass Alan (whom she insists on calling Alain) and keeps insisting that they meet. She also keeps asking him why he left her. We are never allowed to perceive Alan's thoughts, and when he talks about Claude with his male friends, he pretends that he does not know what she wants from him.

These meetings then converge into a moment of mystery when, in chapter IX, Claude asks Alan "What happened?" (Josipovici 2009: 83), referring to "That day" (83), and he goes white (84). She then demands: "Alain, she says, Did you think I was dead?" (84). It emerges that he has repressed the events. What happened was that they were in a car, swerved on the sand at the beach, and that she drove away in the car and left him behind. In the text we get seven versions of what happened to cause the accident and how and why she left. These versions are incompatible and the truth is never established. Chapter XI gives us a first version in which Alan says that Claude was driving and failed to slow down. He also claims that she was asleep at the wheel, that he got out of the car to vomit and went towards the sea. She asserts that she felt left for dead and then took the car; he maintains he returned to find the car gone. He did not call her because his father died (93-5). She accuses him of having wanted her dead (96).

In chapter XII it is she who tells the story. She claims that he was driving, that they quarreled and he refused to slow down and caused the accident. She declares that she was thrown out of the car, had blood on her face, lay in the sand for a long time, then failed to find Alan and the car, got lost, and eventually did come upon the car and left (99-101). She proclaims she wanted to find him in England in order to kill him (102), but it is a joke.

In chapter XIII Alan and Claude co-narrate events. In this account there was no accident. They both got out of the car. She went to sleep in the dunes. He took a walk and she was gone when he returned (103-5). During their meeting in the present she insists on their going to the seaside.

In chapter XIV it is again Claude who tells the story. They skidded, got into the dunes, took each other's clothes off and "afterwards" (108) went to sleep. She woke up, felt herself abandoned, and departed when he did not show up (109). In the fifth version in chapter XV she claims that he hit her with his fist on the beach (112-4).

En route to the beach (narrated in chapter XVII) she reverts to his hitting her. Alan in this sixth adaptation claims she had asked him to hit her (121). She now acknowledges that they skidded because he touched her as she(?) was driving and that she wanted him to hit her (121-2). In the final seventh account she is the one to take off her own clothes and then his. She contends that he got afraid of having killed her and that is why he never got back in touch with her. She accuses him of having left her for dead, but in fact she had left with the car, so he knew she was not dead (123).

On the plot level of the fictional present they go to a hotel. After dinner they plan to take a walk on the beach. When he looks for her, she has left. He searches for her on the beach, finally finds her and walks over to her (131). What happens after this is left pending. The last chapter of the novel is set at another party at Sam Susskind's, where Alan learns Claude has again left (returning overseas) without telling him, thus repeating his own gesture of non-communication years ago.

Although Claude does not kill Alan, she obviously retaliates by playing hide and seek with him on the beach and then by disappearing from his life, returning to America. The seven versions of what happened originally are all contradictory, but what emerges as even more confusing is the characters' lack of motive for telling the various lies or fantasies. Is Alan really culpable of violence or not?[7] The most striking feature in the text relates to the banality of Alan's conversations with all and sundry in contrast to the accusation of murder proclaimed by Claude. Alan's everyday life on the surface is extremely trivial, and even his conversations with Claude, down to the sessions in which they reconstruct events on the beach, are more than anodyne in tone, like an interrogation in which Alan does not express any emotions. One wonders whether he is shy, obtuse, or refuses to allow himself to get emotionally involved.

In what follows I would like to analyze two scenes in some detail. The first is an example of what Jonathan Beckman in his review has called

Josipovici's "frothy, cocktail-party" mode of dialogue: "Josipovici is especially good not only when gently satirising the self-regard, banality and indirection of such chit-chat, but also in recognising that this is the only way we have of finding out about those we do not know, and unlocking the secrets of those we do" (Beckman 2011).

> — There was really no need for you to come, Ronnie Chinn says.
> — I wanted to, Alan says.
> Ronnie Chinn stands in the open doorway. He passes a hand over his face.
> — How are you? Alan asks.
> — You'd better come in, Ronnie Chin says.
> They stand in the hall.
> — Traffic was terrible, Alan says.
> — It always is, Ronnie Chinn says. He shuts the door and locks it.
> — Would you like some coffee? he asks. (Josipovici 2009: ch. V, 49)

> Ronnie Chinn wanders off towards the kitchen.
> — Do you want me in the kitchen? Alan asks.
> — What? Ronnie Chinn says.
> — Shall I come in with you while you make the coffee?
> — Oh yes, Ronnie Chinn says. Please.
> They stand in the kitchen.
> Alan sits at the kitchen table, Ronnie Chinn stands looking out of the window.
> — How are things? Alan asks.
> — What?
> — I wondered how you were coping.
> — Terrible, Ronnie Chinn says. I feel terrible all the time.

Alan is silent.

— I've felt terrible ever since Jane left me, Ronnie Chinn says.

Ronnie Chinn fills the kettle and plugs it in.

— Doesn't the work help? Alan asks.

— I feel terrible at work, Ronnie Chinn says.

He stares down at the kettle, which is beginning to make a noise.

— And then with my father dying, he says.

— He had a good life, Alan says.

The kettle comes to the boil and then switches itself off.

— Nothing prepares you for these things, he says.

Alan sits in silence.

— He had a miserable life, Ronnie Chinn says. Ever since my mother died.

He takes a tin of Nescafé out of the cupboard and stands, holding it in his hand. (50)

Alan and Ronnie seem to exchange banalities, but the two men try to talk about their emotions in an acceptably distanced manner. Ronnie cannot get over his desertion by Jane, and Alan tries to sympathize. Their clichéd exchange is off-puttingly trivial, yet there is artistry in the way in which cliché is piled on cliché, since this reflects the manner in which both interlocutors are helpless in the face of grief and the exposure of their own vulnerability.[8] On Alan's side, his attempt to cajole Ronnie into a semblance of normality by means of pious commonplaces is motivated by his unwillingness to make Ronnie lose face. In the book we learn nothing of Alan's real thoughts—the surprise of meeting Claude again is indicated only by "Alan stares at her" (11) and "He doesn't move" (12) and twice again "He stares at her" (12) and "He stares" (12); the shock he experiences conveys itself even to his host:

> Sam Susskind looks up from his bottles and stares at
> him.
> — Are you all right? he asks.
> — Yes. Why?
> — I don't know. You . . . I didn't fuck up, did I? (16)

Obviously, Alan has been badly shaken and looks it—did he really think she was dead?

Using dialogue in this manner resembles an experience as if one were to hear film dialogue without the screen images and their give-away facial expressions and gestures. Josipovici forces the reader to imagine, but leaves him in the dark:

> To be human is to be amongst those whose thoughts we don't we [sic] know; to be in the dark. Perhaps this condition is the source of our urge to speak. Language, born of absence, filling a lack, generating light. To be human is to be alone, and also to know that we are in thrall to thoughts we call our own, yet are barely aware of. Perhaps this very unknowingness is the source of writing. Writing from out of a void, to fill a void. Both speaking and writing, then, veil ignorance of ourselves and of others even as they display it, even as they ameliorate it. (Thwaite 2011)

The wonder is that such minimalism resonates with significance.[9] Had we left a tape-recorder in the kitchen, the dialogue might have run just like that. Unlike the Victorian novel, where such situations of embarrassment are camouflaged by full sentences honed rhetorically to convey sentiments of propriety and elegance, Josipovici's reductionism underlines the ultimate impossibility of communicating with others on a level of emotional engagement.

Josipovici's dialogue seems to be a very male manner of verbal exchange, of the flight from commitment and emotional engagement, yet he also uses it to delineate small talk with female party guests and to sketch the embarrassed exchanges between Alan and Claude. However, the dialogues with Claude develop to move into different registers. On the one hand, we get Claude as the slightly menacing stalker who keeps contacting Alan:

> — Alain?
> — Yes.
> — It's me. Claude.
> — I know.
> — I left a message, Alain. I asked you to call me back.
> — I know. Sarah passed it on. I've been very busy, Claude.
> — You've been avoiding me.
> — Not at all.
> — You hoped I didn't really exist, didn't you, Alain? she says. You hoped you'd only imagined me.
> — Not at all.
> — It doesn't matter, she says. I told you it didn't matter. Once I had you at the end of my line.
>> He is silent. (32)

> — Claude, he says, are you sure you want us to meet?
> — Of course, she says. That's what I've come here for.
> — Don't be silly.
> — I have. Honest.
>> He is silent. Then he says: — I don't know what you mean.
> — It doesn't matter, she says. She begins to laugh.
> — I have to go, Claude, he says.
> — No, you don't, she says. That's always your first reaction: I have to go. Why can't you talk to me?

— I am talking to you.
— Properly, she says. (34-5)

This exchange prepares us for her increasingly accusatory stance towards Alan, and it demonstrates how she tries to menace him (echoing a Pinteresque heroine). Alan himself is trying to avoid meeting her, but gets cajoled into fixing a date. It is very apparent in the entire novel that Alan is not ruthless enough to simply tell Claude to leave him in peace.

When Claude has finally overcome Alan's resistance to talk about "that day" (83), the reconstructions of the various versions that they tell to one another contrast a very vituperative Claude and a placid and apologetic Alan. He insists that he came back to the car and found it gone. While she keeps returning to the fact that he never called her, the reader may wonder why he was not angry at her for having left him on the beach, when it must have taken him quite some time to get home without a car. In fact, we never hear how he managed to return to the hotel or home. It would even have been quite probable for him to have left his jacket and therefore wallet in the car, in which case renting a car to drive home or paying the hotel bill would have caused numerous problems. (All this happened before the omnipresence of cell phones.) Alan's obvious reluctance to engage with Claude could thus also be motivated by his annoyance with her, an anger which he is much too polite (or perhaps arrogant) to voice.

Summarizing my remarks on *After*, I would like to underline that Josipovici takes his earlier emphasis on existential alienation into greater psychological depth by forcing the readers to imagine motivations for a dialogic exchange that is deliberately bland. The dialogue can also be interpreted as a camouflage for the fact that one's memories and emotions are better left unexpressed or can be expressed only in the fictive exploratory manner in which Alan and Claude keep narratively revisiting and elaborating their Freudian primal scene of violence and treachery. In *Making Mistakes*, the tone is much lighter and the comedy— reminiscent of Mozart's *Così fan tutte* (Waxman 2010; Thwaite 2011)—more traditional in its reference to love and marriage relationships that go astray.

I again start with a plot summary. *Making Mistakes* takes its title phrase from the ending in which Tony tells Bea he made a mistake when he did not marry Bea but her sister Dorothy. The phrase is also used by Tony in his talk with Alfonso when he admits that taking up with his secretary was "a mistake" (ch. xvi; 2009: 228). The novel starts with a dinner party in the house of Dorothy and Tony, with Deirdre and Alfonso and Henriette and Nigel as guests. Bea calls Tony on the phone and says she wants to leave Charlie because he has had yet another affair. The liaison, we learn, is with Angie, who works in a glove shop and is writing a PhD thesis on Poussin, though she does not seem to advance with it.

At the dinner party and in Tony and Dorothy's dialogue when the guests have gone, Dorothy is very dismissive of Bea and her lack of spine in not divorcing Charlie because he keeps betraying her. But then Tony suddenly disappears. Dorothy is worried; she eventually contacts a detective, meeting Charlie (who has been to see Angie) in the café across from the detective agency. Meanwhile, Bea runs into Tony and is sad to learn that he and Dorothy have split up because he had an affair with his secretary Lola Whitehead. At the bottom of his decision to leave was less the affair with Lola (of whom he is now thoroughly sick) but his frustration with his marriage, in which he felt that he could not measure up to Dorothy's standards. In the end, the couples have changed partners, a state of affairs finalized in Tony's conversation with Bea about their meeting in Kew Gardens and subsequent "mistakes" or errors in their choice of partners. It emerges that originally Tony was dating Bea, but then he encountered Dorothy and fell in love, as Bea did with Charlie. Alfonso managed this swap (ch. xxiii). The novel concludes with a dinner party at Deirdre's and Alfonso's at which Tony and Bea are also guests. During dinner they get a phone call from Dorothy saying she is off to Hawaii with Charlie. In the very last chapter we observe Angie (now left behind by Charlie) acquiring a new lover in Lionel (whom we have met having an affair with Bea in ch. xii).

The novel is again very savvy in its presentation of human psychology, but here the characters themselves discuss their psychological problems with some perspicacity. Thus, at the initial dinner party, Bea's and Charlie's rocky marriage is explained as a routine of breaking up and getting together again, and Dorothy's dismissive comments about their marriage provide a good explanation for her way of later dealing with Tony's disappearance. Likewise, Tony's explanation to Alfonso of his problems with Dorothy comes across as a highly convincing analysis of his marriage and Dorothy's hold over him:

> — I look back and think of those fifteen wasted years
> with Dot. Of all the humiliation I endured.
> — There was Sam, Alfonso says.
> — Of course. There was Sam.
> — Don't forget Sam.
> — No. You're quite right. And she had style. You can't
> say she [Dorothy] didn't have style. That's why I fell in
> love with her. For her style. Her imperiousness. Her
> sense that she knew exactly what she wanted out of
> life.
> — You still love that, Alfonso says.
> — I still love that, Tony says.
> — But you find it humiliating to be with her.
> — Yes. (229)

Tony cannot live up to Dorothy's high standards and by failing them in signal manner, he tries to avoid his bad conscience, but things do not work out that way.

Alfonso, who is a professor of psychology (230), gives Tony a series of good pieces of advice. In those passages the dialogue, which started with the party chitchat in chapter I, moves into a humorous but quite insightful delineation of the problems faced by partners who have split up.

Making Mistakes is not only an update on Mozart's opera, it could be treated as a piece of music on account of its symmetrical structure and the way in which various themes are interbraided with one another. There are the partner exchanges, the parallel between the opening and closing dinner parties, the almost farcical manner in which Dorothy runs into Charlie and Bea into Tony, and the rather hilarious knotting together of Lionel and Angie, which disposes of the two outside partners of the previous adulteries. The only person unaccounted for is poor Mrs. Whitehead, the secretary whom Tony has used to get away from Dorothy (a common procedure in marriages that split up).

The passage I would like to discuss in some detail is the following:

> — Things are still difficult between us, he [Charlie] says.
> — They always have been, she [Dorothy] says, laughing suddenly, regaining her composure.
> — Have they?
> — Well, haven't they?
> — Is that what she's told you?
> — She [Bea] doesn't confide in me. You know that.
> — She feels you're always judging her.
> — I am.
> — She feels she can't live up to your high moral standards.
> — She can't.
> — Still so absolute?
> — How can one change, Charlie? At our time of life?
> — That's what keeps us together, he says. We know neither of us can change. Not really. (185-6)

In this conversation Charlie is talking to Dorothy about her sister Bea and their relationship. Charlie laments that his marriage is on the rocks, but Dorothy opines that they have always had a rocky relationship.

Charlie then accuses Dorothy of being judgmental (which we know is true from the opening of the novel), and then Dorothy goes on to deliver a self-satisfied assessment of character remaining unchangeable as one ages. In her case, this is an excuse for holding on to her "high moral standards", but Charlie neatly appropriates this doctrine to his own purposes by claiming that this impossibility of change applies also to his marital relationship—both Bea and himself like to change, and persist in this preference: changeability (or fickleness) is their true character which they have been preserving over the years. Given the ending of the novel, Dorothy's prim confidence in the timelessness of moral character and in the certitude of her own convictions emerge as dramatic ironies: caught up by Tony's desertion, she will start a relationship with Charlie, completely throwing her beliefs overboard (how could she fall in love with Charlie who so signally violated her moral norms?). She even ends up revising her unflattering assessment of Charlie's character.

Making Mistakes, then, develops Josipovici's art of dialogue into a newer and psychologically felicitous dimension. Although the social chitchat and the lack of communication between interlocutors still play a key role in the text, passages that explore the characters' cognition and emotions are foregrounded and provide access to their psychology for the reader. The novel moreover intensifies Josipovici's analysis of quotidian banality, of the everyday social exchange which Marcin Stawiarski has so masterfully examined in his contribution to the 2014 special issue on Josipovici in the online journal *Revue LISA* (Stawiarski 2014b). According to Stawiarski, Josipovici fabricates the "ordinaire", which paradoxically appears undescribable, unsayable, but at the same time exposes hidden meanings, hides its secrets and brings them to our attention.[10] Although we still have to read between the lines and interpret what we 'hear' on the page, the impressions derived from the reading experience convey a new depth and produce an emotional impact. In his more recent writing, then, Gabriel Josipovici has become more accessible and less austere in his modernism, wooing us with his humorous acknowledgement of human fallibility and of life's absurdities. Life à la Josipovici looks less bleak now; there is an attractive streak of wryness in these texts which combines with genuine sympathy for the characters, who therefore appear to us as more real than in earlier texts by the same author. Werner Wolf, commenting on "new trends" in Josipovici's writing, concludes that "[t]his unmistakable quality of Josipovici's stories [...] is [...] the product of a subtle variation of narrative means and an ongoing creative performance leading to ever fresh and sometimes surprising solutions" (Wolf 2014: 25). It pays to read Josipovici now more than ever before.

Endnotes

1 See Finkle (1985), Weatherby (1998), Harms (2000) and Michalzik (2000).

2 See Imhof (1987) and Fludernik (2000).

3 See Josipovici (1983: 177 and 1989: 80).

4 See Fludernik (2000).

5 See also the superb article by Stawiarski (2014b, esp. paragraphs 10-38) on Josipovici's dialogues.

6 Stawiarski (2014b: paragraph 86) also comments on the satiric slant of the novel's opening: "On décèle alors un regard satirique porté sur cet ordinaire banal comme dans ce début mondain de *After* [...]".

7 The prevalence of mysteries or puzzles in Josipovici's oeuvre and its "marked tendency towards contradictions and even paradoxes" has been noted by Wolf (2014: 4).

8 Stawiarski (2014b: paras 10-18) characterizes Josipovici's dialogue as typically determined by three features: (a) incompletion; (b) the taking for granted of information not necessarily accessible to the reader; and (c) redundancy (or repetition).

9 On Josipovici's minimalism see also Wolf (2014: 3), who links it to "one of his principal aesthetic tendencies", a "reductionism" that also produces "an effect of fragmentation" (*ibid.*).

10 See "L'ordinaire paraît indicible, indescriptible, innommable, mais, surtout, il renverse, par l'évidence, le sens cache" (para 4). This analysis is confirmed by Josipovici's own views: "Most of the important feelings we

have are too deep and complex for words—the feeling of loss, for example, or elation. Or ordinary little things like the effect of sunlight on a brick wall as one walks by. If one is struck by something like that—a big thing like the loss of a loved person, a small thing like sunlight on a brick wall—one wants to find a way of expressing that. It's not easy. But it's the only thing that interests me" (Stawiarski 2014a: para 36).

Works Cited

Beckman, Jonathan (2011) 'Review: *After & Making Mistakes. Unhappiness of Being Comfortable*'. *The Jewish Chronicle Online* (18.02.2011). http://www.thejc.com/arts/books/19823/review-after-making-mistakes (accessed 6 January 2016)

Finkle, David (1995) 'What We've Got Here is Failure to Communicate'. *Trenton Times*, Trenton, NJ (16 July 1995), n.p.

Fludernik, Monika (2000) *Echoes and Mirrorings: Gabriel Josipovici's Creative Oeuvre*. Frankfurt: Peter Lang.

Imhof, Rüdiger (1987) 'Gabriel Josipovici'. *Der experimentelle englische Roman der Gegenwart*. Ed. Rüdiger Imhof and Annegret Maack. Tübingen: Francke. 187-208.

Harms, Ingeborg (2000) 'Weil ich ihn nicht mag. Gabriel Josipovici's Roman *Jetzt*'. Frankfurter Allgemeine Zeitung (FAZ) (21 March, 2000): L21.

Josipovici, Gabriel (1983) 'Conclusion: From the Other Side of the Fence, or True Confessions of an Experimentalist'. *The Mirror of Criticism: Selected Reviews, 1977-1982*. Brighton: Harvester Press. 173-180.

Josipovici, Gabriel (1989) 'Writing, Reading, and the Study of Literature'. *New Literary History* 21 (1989-1990): 75-95.

Josipovici, Gabriel (2009) *Two Novels: After & Making Mistakes*. Manchester: Carcanet.

Michalzik, Peter (2000) 'Was ist jetzt'. Süddeutsche Zeitung (28 March 2000): 20.

Stawiarski, Marcin (2014a) 'Interview with Gabriel Josipovici'. *Revue LISA/LISA e-journal* 12.2 (2014). http://lisa.revues.org/5870

Stawiarski, Marcin (2014b) "Gabriel Josipovici et la fabrique de l'ordinaire." *Revue LISA/LISA e-journal* 12.2 (2014). http://lisa.revues.org/5805

Thwaite, Mark (2011) "*After & Making Mistakes*: A Review." http://www.readysteadybook.com/Blog.aspx?tag=gabriel+josipovici (6 April 2011)

Waxman, Jeff (2010) "Review *After & Making Mistakes*." *Review of Contemporary Fiction* (1 April 2010). http://www.readperiodicals.com/201004/2015145891.html

Weatherby, Iain (1998) "Tea and Talk." *Times Literary Supplement* No. 4968 (19 June, 1998): 26.

Wolf, Werner (2014) "'Revealing what cannot be spoken'—Gabriel Josipovici's Short Stories as Illustrations of Transcendental Negativity." *Revue LISA/LISA e-journal* 12.2 (2014). https://lisa.revues.org/5772

VP Review of the Year 2015

GARLAND OSPREY

January to March

Hello, friends! I am Garland Osprey, professional loafer. If you will permit a digression (before we have even begun), let me sketch a concise portrait of the making of me. At the age of nine, I inherited the fortune of Madame Rampart IV, a boiled rice heiress (niece of Uncle Ben), after a chance encounter on the streets of Falkirk. Madame was on one of her visits to unimpressive towns with no notable characteristics when I warned her of a falling 'T' from a café sign. She leapt towards a plumber from East Lothian as the 'T' cracked onto a paving slab and fell facewards. From that moment, I was the most important person in her life (having lost her relatives in a series of quinoa accidents). I inherited her $9,000,000 fortune, and now spend my days having improbable adventures in various locales in the universe, reading a selection of the annum's new releases, a selection of which I will mention in the paragraphs that follow at the behest of Verbi Press.

I commenced the annum in a toboggan in Naples. The perfect location to read *Time Ages in a Hurry* by Antonio Tabucchi, published by **Archipelago**. The nine stories in this volume floated past like the melancholic drift of a shoegazing album (something in the Slowdive or Cocteau Twins range)—an inviting sequence of long breakless paragraphs with short clauses spiralling from speaker to narrator, tripping the light fantastic along the commas until their unhurried stop. Famous for exploring the concept of *saudade*, a popular tone in Portuguese literature of epic nostalgia and yearning for the never-was, the what-is-lost, the can't-remember-ever-having and so on, the ur-text of which is Pessoa's tear-drenched masterplea, *The Book of Disquiet*, Tabucchi in his final published collection before his terminal cancer in 2012, continued his subtle burrowing into the human and European psyche in these nomadic, nation-hopping tales in search of a named character, often overt in their politics but always personal, touching, and—that perfect descriptor—*elegiac*. I was in fine spirits for some summer tobogganing in Naples. I set a new track record of over nine miles per hour and won the cup.

On the plane to Minsk, I read *Blood Brothers* by Ernst Haffner, from **Other Press**—a matter-of-fact, no-nonsense account of teenage tearaways, first published in 1932 and banned by the Nazi Party in 1933. Following a cast of delinquents in their misadventures in the down-and-out, Haffner's novel will appear tame to modern audiences due to the censorship restrictions, however, it is unflinching in its descriptions of teenage prostitution and violence. Making minor use of over-the-shoulder third-person narration to bring the reader closer to the minds of his protagonists, Haffner fails at psychological depth, but brings a social worker's passion and meticulous eye to an otherwise quite straightforward first and last novel. A future as an important socially-conscious voice erased by his disappearance in the 1940s. I managed to squeeze in *White Hunger* by Aki Ollikainen from **Peirene Press**: a Finnish novella set during a 1867 famine that maintains a tone of snow-capped hopelessness without reprieve. Not unlike Andrey Zvyaginstev's recent Russian epic, *Leviathan*, this novel is an unrelenting showcase of the blizzards of unfairness that visit the planet's less fortunate mortals, leaving the reader drenched in gloom and life-loathing. In addition, I read Raymond Jean's *Reader for Hire*. This short novel is hard to pass comment on: a light breeze, a soft squeeze, a cracker with cheese, all these, if you please, I hate to tease, so . . . An attractive woman visits various homes and reads passages from Maupassant, Marx (Karl), Perec, and Pope Clement VII to a wheelchaired teenager, an eccentric Marxist-aristocrat, a sex-starved corporate loon, and a small child deprived of amusement, and attempts to engage her readees in the act of being readed. The novel features no pat lessons on the wondrous transcendence of reading (which might have been welcome), but focuses instead on whimsical comedy, and the heroine's often smug superiority to everyone else, which proves amusing for the short duration. Regardless of the mirth, I arrived in Minsk depressed.

I was there to act as temporary Mayor, having accepted a kind offer from the previous incumbent Sergei Clarkson, who had to leave the nation for a week on urgent business. I was welcomed by the secretary, and began to read that week's briefs. These proved boring. I read instead *The Deep Zoo* by Rikki Ducornet, from **Coffee House Press**. For those seeking a Gass-deep collection of long lingering literary essays, the short-form probing of Rikki Ducornet will not suffice—however, Rikki's *Deep Zoo* is thought-provoking selection of miniatures, bright with her usual preoccupations—Islam and Arabic languages, Gaston Bachelard, Lewis Carroll, the Cabinet of Curiosities, Marquis de Sade, *et al.* Her titular piece on the creative process reveals her own belief in the magic or transgressive aspect of writing (no Gass-long syntax analyses here), using mini-quotes in a commendable effort to describe something that reaches beyond words. There are three tributes to artists (Margie McDonald, Linda Okazaki, Anne Hirondelle), including several pages of examples of their art (taking up a fair percentage of a 107-page book). 'Books of Natural and Unnatural Nature' is a brilliant exploration of Rikki's interest in the natural world and the arcane, and her iconoclastic interests have their manifesto in 'The Practice of Obscurity'. Elsewhere, there are wanderings through Herzog and Lispector ('Houses on Fire'), a minuscule look at her Elements Quartet 'Water and Dreams', a 9/11 response ('War's Body'), *120 Days of Sodom* ('Silling'), William Gass ('A Cup and a River'), David Lynch ('Witchcraft by a Picture'). The charming 'Memoir in the Form of the Manifesto' and 'Candles of Ink' are the closest things in here to straight autobio. A pleasing collection for enthusiasts, and like *The Monstrous and the Marvellous*, leaves our stomachs crying out for more.

Over that relaxing week, I also read *Me, Margarita* by Georgian author Ana Kordzaia-Samadashvili from **Dalkey Archive**. For those not in possession of a wall-map, a hardback atlas, or a rotating globe lamp, Georgia is an East European nation south-west of Russia, north-east of Turkey, bordering Armenia and Azerbaijan, and masks a secret wellspring of terrific fiction from past and present, some of which is being made available via new translations from Dalkey Archive. Having situated these stories on the world map, the difficult task remains situating these stories on the literary map, for the author's tone and humour proved a pest to assimilate (can we detect the dark humour of East Europe, the fierce fairytaling of Western Asia, or the grim satire of Russia?), leading to a frustrating if not unfun hotchpotch of the bracketed elements. AK-S is at her most amusing when taking up the blunt and dark humour of 'Berikaoba' or 'Nina', tales relating the complex relationships of terrific female terrors. Most of these stories deal in abstract and unusual ways with the nuances of Georgian emotional (and unemotional) relationships, and have a knowing scalpel-sharp wit to them, if sometimes the content and conclusions seem a little flat or head-scratching.

From that same publisher, the startling *Kvachi* by Mikheil Javakhishvili. First written as a series of sketches and reworked into a novel, *Kvachi* was published in 1925, a year after the author evaded execution for supporting the socialist party, and less fortunate writers met the brunt of the Communist uprising. A long-buried Georgian classic in the picaresque mould of Cervantes and Fielding with a nod towards the French decadents, *Kvachi* is an exhausting stop-start rags-to-riches-to-rags tale featuring the titular confidence trickster, whose talent for hoodwinking the common to the noble knows no limitations, and whose skill for evading the noose in even the most improbable of circumstances borders on divine providence. Kvachi's adventures commence in Georgia, migrate to Russia in the court of Rasputin (to whom K becomes friend and confidante), and take in the extravagance of Paris and chaos of Communist Europe, where the more interesting historical comment is housed in a novel devoid of such frill as psychological depth or critical volleys towards the regimes of the time (the author was tortured for two months during the Great Terror of 1937, then executed—his reticence to 'speak out' is understandable), although the depiction of Kvachi's life was shocking and provocative for the era. The figure of the self-made scoundrel is popular in Georgia and other East European countries, having a famous bedfellow in Jaroslav Hašek's hilarious *The Good Soldier Švejk*, published in Czech in 1923. Kvachi fast descends into a sequence of scrapes and their (sometimes) positive outcomes (there are several macabre murder and torture scenes), and often lacks of the coherence of a proper novel (as a series of sketches might do), but always leaves the reader rooting for the scoundrel in spite of his sins, and the fast-paced dialogue, black humour, and camaraderie-among-thieves keeps the antics fun and ingenious for the duration. Recommended for fans of daring and rebellious literature.

Before I left (following an intense spat over the closure of a commuter bridge with local architect Vladimir Wilson), I read Louis Bury's *Exercises in Criticism*. His ambitious intention was to mimic Queneau's *Exercises in Style* in criticism, with each critical piece mimicking its topic—his original dissertation containing 99 pieces and over 600 pages. This skinnier version contains barely over thirty of his exercises, and while an entertaining and original conceit, seems fairly incoherent. Ranging from short Oulipo homages (an excellent condensed take on Queneau's *Exercises*), an N+7, and a fiddle with Mathews's masturbation collection *Singular Pleasures*, to tributes and discussions on various overlooked North American "post-Oulipo" productions, such as Sorrentino's interrogatory masterpiece *Gold Fools* (written in questions, of course), Doug Nufer's novels *Negativeland* and *Never Again* (no positives or repeated words), and poetic productions by Darren Wershler-Henry, Harryette Mullan, and Dodie Bellamy, to more personal (and oft baffling) material such as a Q+A with his Polish-immigrant father, and 70+ pages of transcriptions from his grandmother's notebooks, the collection seems to derail entirely from its more interesting critical aims, falling instead into a "personal" project that doesn't particularly wed the constraint-investigations harmoniously with his Holocaust backdrop in homage to Perec. The explanations preceding each chapter are very appealing however, and his own self-interrogations are illuminating insights into his intentions, making the reader sympathetic with the shifting nature of the project, regardless if the end result seems ultimately unsatisfying. A compelling book, certainly the first of its kind in the scholarly field.

Sergei was pleased with the inaction I had shown as Mayor of Minsk. "Better to be inert than inept," he remarked. I had been both inert and inept. The two were often mutually exclusive, but I kept this observation to myself. On the plane home, I read *The Dream of my Return* by Horacio Castellanos Moya, from **New Directions**. The Latin American novel is rife with rambling first-person narrators prone to digressions and seeming plot dead-ends (see the maestros Infante and Bolaño for more), and this short entertaining novel continues in that tradition with a frenetic narrator receiving treatment for his nerves from doctor Don Chente as his marriage decomposes, and his rage towards his wife's lover rises to a murderous pitch, and a sequence of other events occur of varying interest as he plans his return to El Salvador at the end of the civil war. Not as humorous as the blurb indicates, not a patch on Mr. Bernhard, but pleasing for the two hours reading time.

I also read *Coyote* by Colin Winnette from **Les Figues Press**. A novella pre-loaded with epic emotional trauma, purely by dint of its topic (missing child) and focus (parents of missing child), this book has little work to do in wringing as much pathos and empathy for its protagonists as possible, although is not averse to cranking the trauma knob with occasional overblown scenes of hysteria (half-mad mother setting fire to her house, assaulting security guard). Told in flat and often awkward prose, this novella seems more concerned with mining as much emotional trauma from the scenario as possible, and as a consequence, feels like an exercise in audience manipulation like so much fiction in this mode.

Back home in Falkirk, I read *The Dirty Dust* by Máirtín Ó Cadhain, one of the annum's best discoveries, from **Yale University Press.** A classic of the Irish language, a lost modernist epic, Ó Cadhain's novel has been published in English translation for the first time, rendered in all its foul splendour by novelist Alan Titley. A multitude of voices from beyond the grave narrate this fantastically obscene novel, led by the histrionic Caitriona Puadeen, forever battling idle tittle-tattle about her character from the longer-dead residents of the cemetery. A frenetic stream of insults, hearsay, banter, prattle, and bickering, the novel flits from one unidentified voice to another (Caitriona stands out with her oft-used catchphrase "I'm going to burst!"), split into ten sections with occasional lyrical turns from the Trumpet of the Graveyard, showcasing Ó Cadhain's talent for language (outside the inventive curses and epithets—the scriptwriters of *The Thick of It* might find themselves blushing). Ó Cadhain was a fierce trumpeter of the Irish language, controversial for writing in the vernacular of ordinary Irish people with no fear of the censor, and remained untranslated for decades due to the text's problematic (and dated) slang usage. Dense in allusions to the politics and references of the period (late 1940s), Yale Press plan to release a second annotated translation in 2016, for those interested in further context or outright scholarship. A second novel, *The Key*, a Kafkaesque comic monologue, has been published by **Dalkey Archive**—constituting something of a revival for this writer who might in time find himself mentioned in the same breath as O'Brien or Beckett. In the meantime, this blackly funny novel can be read for its wicked humour and sublime Irish banter by the plain-drinking masses, who may never see its like again. The last word to Caitriona: "You can go fuck off, you old bags. No one of yours ever had a good word to say, ever . . . Shag off, this is not your grave anyway . . . The graveyard must be all over the bleedin' gaff if they put you into the same grave as me. Shag off to the Half Guinea Place. Did you hear about the altar I had? Did you hear what the priest said about me? Your coffin never went beyond five pounds. You can go and fuck off."

March to May

Back home, I fell into a spell of depression and took to soaking in a bath several times per afternoon and munching overlong hotdogs. To lift me from this slump, I read works from the smashing **Open Letter Press**. First, *Post-Exoticism in Ten Lessons, Lesson Eleven* by Antoine Volodine. This curious French writer, adopting multiple *noms de plumes*, has embarked upon an ambitious undertaking—the invention of a new school of writing known as "post-exoticism", of which this is a mini-manifesto of sorts, containing its own set of opaque conceptual parameters, as outlined in ten parts alongside a strange dark narrative taking place within the compound where these writers are imprisoned. The school of "post-exoticism" is a fertile collective of writers united under the same rubric, parameters, oppressions, whose style, if this novella is an accurate representative, is a mix of Borges's droll academia, Édouard Levé's lists and fragments, Kafka's paranoia, and a form of highfalutin humourless nonsense. Like the Dalkey release *Writers*, this short work packs in hundreds of weird ideas and scenarios, most of them unfathomable, and some inventive book titles that eclipse the work's own, and falls into a rut of straight-faced opaque oddballery that can be tiresome to read.

Next came *The Physics of Sorrow* by George Gospodinov. This sprawling and brilliant new work from the Bulgarian maverick responsible for the "novel about nothing" (not his words), *Natural Novel*, returns in English with a novel that has "career-defining" stamped all over (not on the cover). A rich exploration of the author's family history, the Minotaur myth, the physics of elementary particles, the author's own melancholies, socialism, vegetarianism, and boredom in Bulgaria, and quirky absent friends, narrated in numerous novel and hilarious and moving voices, retaining the fast-paced tale-spinner feel throughout and entertaining from first to the last, this is a no-brainer purchase.

The novel that lifted me from this sadness: *Lies, First Person* by Gail Hareven. A provocative novel from the Hebrew exploring the impact of a sister's childhood rape on a newspaper columnist and her husband. The rapist, known as the 'Not-Man' is protagonist Elinor's uncle, and after time in exile in America, is due to appear in Jerusalem repenting a first-person autobiography of Hitler, and perhaps his earlier crimes. The novel is readable with its straightforward prose and thought-provoking themes (not unlike those middlebrow 'dilemma' novels in this language), although its focus on the protagonist's detailed feelings and opinions on her uncle, her sister, her husband, her column's heroine (a "pigtail-sucker", we are told 1000+ times), and all other aspects of her life means the reader has to beg the narrator's indulgence often (and question when she is fibbing or not, or if it matters), and proceed in spite of her repetitions, and the standoffish and humourless tone.

I booked a ticket to Nuuk in Greenland. On the plane, I read Yuri Herrera's *Signs Preceding the End of the World* from **And Other Stories.** Sometimes us readers find ourselves drowning in superlatives, in the fawning pith clipped to the front and back and inside pages of new literature, forcing us to retreat into the hallowed recesses of the obscure, sniffing for unpraised truffles amid the chaff, and in most cases these superlatives raise our expectations to ludicrous levels before the cover has been admired or the blurb has been scanned, causing outrage at the over-pumped words that writers and critics are obligated to dole out from term to term to keep the pretence alive that Fresh and New and Vital Literature is still being written (if not the Grants and Council Funding will stop!), and the inevitable disappointment at not being taken to the Nirvana that James Kirkenhead at *Kirkus Reviews* promised on the backflap. That is one cross we have to bear as readers. This lean and intelligent novella earns its superlatives (and yes, perhaps this anti-superlative preface is in itself a superlative, however, at least this anti-superlative-superlative avoids the words "stunning" and "greatest" in a sincere sentence, and perhaps even pricks your disinterest).

May to August

I spent an outrageous summer in the bustling environment of Nuuk. Famed for its all-night raves, sacrificial ceremonies of hemp and crossword puzzles to the Emperor, and jug band dance-offs, this place kept me more than occupied. I managed to poke around in the pages of

FC2. I read *Seed* by Stanley Crawford. A new Stanley Crawford novel is an event, celebrated in my neighbourhood with all-night raves and intense cheese-and-nibble comedowns around 4am. His previous novel, the tender satire (this phrase perhaps defines his oeuvre) *Petroleum Man*, explored the trickledown effect of laissez-faire capitalism on the family, and in *Seed*, Crawford once again deals with material things and their impact upon the soul. Bill Starr is spending his twilight alone, following the loss of his wife some time earlier, with his nagging Mexican carer who hopes to inherit the possessions her boss has begun auctioning off to his remaining relations. Having summoned his relatives to claim their inheritances, Bill bumbles around his house welcoming his thrice-removed nephews and nieces, misremembering their names every few minutes, having secret erotic thoughts he hopes he never expresses, and offering them random possessions, including a 1937 convertible to a married couple, which has a deleterious impact on their relationship. This novel is a warm and melancholic rumination on ageing and the eventual worthlessness of a life's amassed possessions when knocking on heaven's door.

And next, *Theories of Forgetting* by Lance Olsen. Lance Olsen is the Anthony Burgess of his time and place, producing novels, short story collections, and non-fiction books at an impressive rate, and like Bugress, has a fondness for restless innovation and risky exploration. Unlike Burgess, Olsen seems to succeed in creating more unique and lasting works, and favours a less frivolous sub-Joycean mode of experiment, embracing technology and breaking down the conventional typesetting of the book. In this novel, much like Benjamin Stein's *The Canvas*, the story can be read from either side (two back covers to choose from), and as in that novel, the topic matter is fairly ordinary—a man has a breakdown after the loss of his wife (whose decline is one of the narratives), and a sister comes to terms with her errant brother, Lance Olsen. The protagonists being artists and literary people, this allows for a more-than-liberal splashing of quotations from artists and writers across its pages and margins, and various photos inserted to accompany the downbeat tone. The female narrative is the most engaging for its doomed brevity, the male narrative and marginalia are less impressive and lack coherence, as does the novel on the whole. Otherwise, a risky and worthwhile subversion of the usual. (Lance also has a piece on Raymond Federman in this thing: *Verbivoracious Festschrift Volume Three: The Syllabus*).

And heading back a few years, but most certainly worth an honorable mention: *Once Human*, by Steve Tomasula. These stories explore the possibilities of narrative to cross-breed visual art with prose, turning in some impressive results. Opener 'The Colour of Flesh' is a feminist fable with manga illustrations from Maria Tomasula where the text is weaved into the art with seamless panache, making each turn of the page an exciting event. 'C-U See-Me' is a less subtle satire on the Big Brother CCTV state-of-the-nation and its visuals pertain (on purpose) to the bland. 'The Color of Pain and Suffering' explores Tomasz's relationship and career as a visual artist working on visceral material and is another highlight. 'The Atlas of Man' is another beautiful piece of work exploring the collection's nub—the eccentricities of science and technologies in relation to the eccentricities of human beings. Duller fare pads out the collection, such as the inexplicable 'The Risk-Taking Gene as Expressed by Some Asian Subjects' and the novella 'Medieval Times'. The latter is the most inventive in terms of content and approach. Closer 'Farewell to Kilmanjaro' ends the book on an elegiac note. A trimmed-down collection might have produced a more satisfying read—regardless this is important and wonderful fiction.

Nuuk is one of the most vibrant places in the universe! During the course of my trip, I attended a nine-hour lecture on the parallels between Desmond Morris and the Manic Street Preachers, met several cocaine dealers who had set up a trust for the preservation of the falcon, an artist famed for his surrealist representations of Nuuk in the winter, and a writer famed for his sequence of erotic foresting novels. Before leaving, I read David Rose's *Meridian* from **Unthank Books.** This impressive second novel from late-starter David Rose concerns an architect and his impressions of the world and his work and, in a similar if less lexilubricious manner to Brooke-Rose's *Amalgamenmon*, makes the "discourses run together", introducing an alphabetised stream of narratives in a form of existential baton-pass and, later in the narrative, bold-faced and italicised sections are weaved into the architect's narration (chock full of informative architectural and etymological trivia) to form a multitude of tongues ("heteroglossia" the blurb boldly proclaims), in an engaging and intricate novel that manages to be simultaneously complex and none-too-tricky to digest and appreciate.

August to October

Back in Falkirk, I set about founding a Society for the Protection of the Falcon. Falcon hunting had tripled in 2014, following the revelation that a falcon's beak is tastier than caviar when boiled. Hunters had been shooting down then tearing off the beaks, leaving the helpless birds to die in pain. I hired 93 workers to man the offices, and on a well-needed week's break (I had saved over 1,828 falcons by Nov 2nd), I read works from **New Directions.** First, *Oreo* by Fran Ross. This early-seventies punnilinguistic mistresspiece deserves a broader readership. An anarchic comedic romp, abounding in ambidextrous wordplay, mixing black and Jewish slang with technical and mathematical language, this novel is a brassy performance, sadomasochistically whip-smart, ferociously intelligent, and unafraid to wipe the smug complicity off your face with a crude or revolting image. Epic in scope (structured around the odyssey of Theseus), *Oreo* is the only novel from a fearless humorist on a par with Ishmael Reed or Mel Brooks. I also read a reissue of Nathalie Sarraute's *Tropisms.* One of the lesser-known pioneers of the nouveau roman, alongside Butor and Robbe-Grillet, this first publication introduces to readers her subtle, moving tone, something she developed in a long and fascinating corpus. As part of their Pearls series (short books in length and dimensions), I also read *Because She Never Asked* from Enrique Vila-

Matas, the latest in a series of this playful, metafictional author's body of exciting and innovative works.

I was awarded a Best Falcon Saver of the Year medal by the Falkirk Council. In addition to this, I was longlisted for the RSPCA Hero of the Year award, but lost out to a grandmother from Cromarty who rescued nine dolphins from an oil spill. To appease the rage, I read works from **Maclehose Press**. The first: *Portrait of a Man*, Georges Perec. This is Perec's "first and last" novel, published in French in 2012. His career began with the superlative *Things: A Story of the Sixties*, a timeless and downbeat satire on conspicuous consumption, and this novel about failed forger and murderer Gaspard Winckler (close cousin of Henry), is a curious, repetitive, and playful work from a 24-year-old Perec still uncovering his powers over the pen. Part One is told in first, second, and third person perspectives (the second-person is used as an interior monologue), and flits to and fro as Winckler's tale is told with unchronological abandon. Part Two is a form of interrogation—a two-way confession in dialogue, switching into first-person narrative later on, and an art catalogue towards the end. This is a busy bit of business, but the frenetic narration mirrors the narrator's post-traumatic mental state, making for a highly engaging and fast-paced novel in the *nouveau roman* mode.

The second: *Parfums: A Catalogue of Smells* by Philippe Claudel. This catalogue of 61 "remembered smells" from the author of *Broderick's Report* is a wistful and sincere slice of page-turning literary gateaux—at once observational and autobiographical, Claudel's smells range from the common (Cabbage: "A sort of identity card of wretchedness"), to pongs (*Pissotières*: "I would come across a certain kind of mirror that didn't distort much. I would learn who I was"), to the homely (Clean sheets: "a vulnerable creature who knows that for the time being he is swathed and happy"), to the morbid (Death: "An odd mixture of formalin and powdered rice, of make-up and camphorated lotion"), to the erotic (Girlfriends: "something vegetable and sugary, candied, a whiff of confectionery, of home-made cakes, of plant stems and open fields"), to further pongs (Sewage works: "you cannot judge a smell by its colour").

The voice here is humorous and sentimental, reflective and revelling—Claudel celebrates a broad range of earthly smells in the Rabelaisian spirit, and produces a short catalogue vibrant with the many nasal wonders that awaits us in the world, inviting us to consider our own madeleines, turn-offs, and nostril-tinglers.

October to December

Leaving the Falcon Society in the capable hands of Michael Arnold, former editor of the *Kestrel Watch Weekly*, a fine periodical on all things kestrel, I went to visit relatives in Senegal. I have two cousins, Kidd and Lode. Their French parents had remained after the French retreat in the 1960s, and established a music school there. I volunteered to help teach local children the bassoon and oboe, my two favourite instruments. In between that, I read some **New York Review Books** releases. The first, *A School for Fools* by Sasha Sokolov. Sokolov's first novel has little of the verbal explosiveness of his opus *Astrophobia*. The novel challenges conventional narrative modes, breaking down the unities of time and place, and obscuring narrator(s) and voices, to the extent the prose becomes a wash of poetic and strange scenes punctuated with tagless dialogue and copious literary and historical references and puns. Dreamlike and unusual and impossible to follow at times. In Russian the prose is more musical (according to other reviews), so it appears this translation is a pleasant attempt but lacks the flowing music of the mother tongue. The second, Emmanuel Bove's *Henri Duchemin and His Shadows*. Bove, famous for his masterpiece of solitude *My Friends*, also penned short paeans to solitude and strange male friendships, seven of which are collected in this fresh translation. 'Night Crime' features a woeful soul whose whisperings lead to murder, a fattened wallet, and the inevitable moral decay; 'Another Friend' a woeful soul who meets a rich 'friend to the poor' who proves to be no friend at all; 'Night Visit' a woeful soul whose girlfriend in a moment of thoughtless cruelty ends their relationship; 'What I Saw' a woeful soul convinced his wife was kissing another man in a taxi; 'The

Story of a Madman' a woeful soul who chooses to sever contact with everyone close to him to make them suffer; 'The Child's Return' a woeful soul who is unable to return to his parental home after a long absence; 'Is it a Lie?' a woeful soul who wonders where his wife was last night. A pattern is clear: woeful souls whose relationships are teetering on the brink of severance, or fail to even occur. The pain of attempting to make meaningful contact with another human being is Bove's topic, one plumbed with wonder here.

In between helping Aaron Emmons with his skiffle concerto, I checked out a few more recent titles from small presses. First, **Stacherone Books**. I read *The Compleat Memoirrhoids* by Steve Katz: an *omnium-gatherum* of Katzland. An abecedarian trek into Steveworld. Steve discusses his travels. Steve waxes on his childhood in Washington Heights. Steve discusses his travels. Steve waxes on his childhood in Washington Heights. Steve mentions *The Exagggerations of Peter Prince* (several times—hinting this is his favourite novel). Steve discusses his travels. And so on. This selection of memoirrhoids is as unreliable, vivid, banal, personal-emotional, and revealing as one's memory tends to be, and Katz doesn't hide the unpleasant parts of his character (prostitutes and affairs), or the missed chances (networking with Vonnegut, Vidal and co), and nor does he inflate his own achievements (shame—Katz is underrate), nor shy away from respecting the artists that made his life a pleasure (more on Federman and Sukenick might have been welcome), and the bulk of the book is devoted to adventures with his first wife, suggesting these were the happiest times (the 1960s, of course).

Next, *Conversations with Stalin* by Eleanor Antin from **Green Integer**. Eleanor Antin is a performance / installation / conceptual artist from the Bronx region and other half of avant-garde poet David (Antin). She also wrote this pseudo-autobiographical caper about a young lady (named Eleanor)'s adventures in the Bronx region among her Polish Stalinist mother and upbringing as a Communist. At the end of each chapter, Eleanor engages in a conversation with Stalin who offers advice befitting his despotic beliefs, plunging her into further eschatological confusion.

This is a small-sized, fast-paced, anecdotal-in-tone work mixing some hilarious and traumatic moments alongside the fantastical. Explore some of her playful-sounding and audacious artworks in the near future.

And from **Visual Editions**, Douglas Coupland's *Kitten Clone: Inside Alcatel-Lucent*. Douglas Coupland's tech-ennui fictions have never appealed to me, lounging on the bland pouffe of lit-fic, lacking in that prose razzle-dazzle so crucial to me, and satirising with sitcom-level humour (not of the *Veep* calibre). This extended essay (magazine article) explores a tedious net-peddling company, and the impact of the web on our psyches and lives (coming to no conclusions except: be worried), in an informative manner, with photos of the bland corporate surroundings suggesting a lurking darkness, written in a down-to-earth style that makes for pleasant and simple reading. No real intellectual substance here, and one longs to read what dear Foster Wallace might have done with such an assignment. This is (in the UK) part of Visual Editions Writers-in-Residence series, where high-profile writers tackle the complex matrices of our corporate dystopia in an amusing manner. A noble aim, except these "books" are like art magazines sold at £25 ($40) per unit, so seem quite steep for the casually curious.

I ended this mixed annum with a spectacular knees-up at the Dakar Concert Hall. Kidd and Lode performed moving oboe and bassoon numbers, and the Aaron Emmons Skiffle Extravaganza treated us to two hours of incredible skiffle melodies. I ended the year reading a fine book about music: Martin Aston's *Facing the Other Way: The Story of 4AD*, from **The Friday Project**. For me, 4AD is to music as Dalkey is to books—an independent label serving up divine music in beautiful packaging—and this thorough account of the label's pivotal first two decades is a perfect reason to dip back into the back catalogue. 4AD's architect was retiring depressive Ivo Watts-Russell, whose taste in artful melancholia led to three This Mortal Coil albums and helped shape their roster. Martin Aston's love for 4AD shines in this respectful account drawn in large part from interviews with the leading players and artists, most of whom have contributed (Kristin Hersh, Frank Black, Kim Deal, Robin Guthrie, Lisa

Germano *et al*), to share their (respectful and adoring) opinions on their time at 4AD. Fascinating is the portrayal of Ivo as the reluctant Svengali, whose skill at transferring his personal demons and sadness into breathtaking and wrenching music seems unparalleled among record labels, and Vaughan Oliver's record sleeve art is discussed with due deference also, as an integral part of the 4AD aesthetic. Short histories of each artist's evolution within the label are also provided, along with accounts of the business's fortunes and misfortunes, making this tome the last word on this magnificent label, still thriving under new ownership and championing challenging new music.

Extra Reads

If I might be permitted a slight indulgence: Adam Thirlwell's *Lurid & Cute* from **Jonathan Cape**. There's that friend of yours, the logorrhoeic loudmouth always on cue with the perfect witticism at the right time, equipped with an anecdote for all occasions (that you suspect he practices in the mirror at home), forever present at all social moments to release another stream of verbal sophistication leaving you cowering in the corner, wondering if you ever learned the alphabet properly, or learned to speak at a post-toddler level, and there's this friend of yours who, after too many drinks, loses control of this verbal prowess, permitting each thought to emerge unedited and to spin on for twelve minutes too long, until everyone round the table begins exchanging desperate glances, checking their phones, and inventing reasons to leave, locked in unspoken battle for the right moment to stand up and flee, until you alone remain in the bar, nodding along to the now incoherent and awkwardly personal material he is unselfconsciously unloading into your ear, allowing you time only to nod or express a syllable of assent or consolation, before you too check your phone and contrive some way of leaving, despite this person being your only real friend, and the one person you admire and respect, and that his lack of awareness around this drunken prattle problem is the one characteristic that endears you to him the most, because you simply envy the pre-drunk society wit side, and that this friendship leaves you unfulfilled, lonely, and increasingly alienated in your very narrow and ultimately tragic life—that person narrates this novel. Proof indeed that small presses produce the finest books.

Before I bid adieu, let me relate a few more titles from **Dalkey Archive** read. First, *Addendum to a Photo Album* by Vladislav Otroshenko. Alas, I almost felt illiterate reading this novella—it seems there was some curious barrier constructed between my eyes, the text, and my comprehension of its content. As I ploughed through another interminable, whimsical sentence about this irritating family (who we are expected to find amusing or charming without the writer having to earn this, as if we have wandered onto the sofa of some overeager prattling auntie desperate to relay another hilarious anecdote about long-dead relatives for another three hours before your train departs), I started to have serious pain in my precious eyeballs. A patchwork of long-winded whimsy, of interest to fans of Cossacks as directed by Wes Anderson.

More fun was had with Warren Motte's *Mirror Gazing*. A book-length essay on mirror scenes in novels structured around a rambling framework. Motte is apologetic and self-conscious about his hobbyist tone, and despite this reader's not being too enthralled with the topic, the book is endearing and incisive in its endeavour, and most crucially, passionately verbivoracious. His decision to include mirror scenes from crime fiction and mass-market potboilers (*Da Vinci Code!*) spoils the proceedings somewhat and upsets this reader on a deeply personal level. Mirbeau is one of the lesser-known decadent writers, famed for his seminal *Torture Garden*. The brilliant new translation of *Twenty-One Days of a Neuraesthenic* from Justin Vicari renders the original in its scabrous and hilarious best. A sequence of stories told by residents of a rest cure resort, relating tales of corruption, hypocrisy, and madness. A terrific novel twice as relevant to these times. Edouard Leve's final novel to be translated into English, *Newspaper*, is a captivating roll of catastrophes, listings, and other nonsense as found in a newspaper. And finally, *Caterva.*

The second novel of Filloy's in English translation following the spectacular *Op Oloop* in 2009, this is a verbose, relentless epic-of-sorts featuring a 'caterva' (i.e. ragbag gang) of misfits prone to deep intellectual ruminations and phonations on their purposeless wanderings. The novel is essentially a vehicle for Filloy's sublime skill with the language (the translation from Brendan Riley reflects this with marvellous turns of phrase around every corner) and impressive range of erudition. As Riley explains in his intro, the novel makes use of "acronyms; newspaper articles and editorials; chiastic syntax; cypher; epic catalogue; entomological monographs; eulogies; gravestone inscriptions; industrial labels; comically illiterate receipts; intimate confessional letters; headlines; parables; parody; pastoral lyricism; paronomasia; portmanteau words; and free-form stream-of-consciousness writing" and mirrors *Ulysses* in its ambitions and scope in terms of the language being used (if not in structure or theme). The shambling nature of the adventures and similar tone of their thoughts and speeches, however, can make reading on wearisome, and the erudition here passes into the long-winded and arcane on occasion, making for a less than exuberant encyclopedic experience. Adieu!

About the Contributors

Peter Blundell was born in Reading. He currently lives and continues to write in South London.

Keith Byerman is a professor of English at Indiana State University. He specializes in African American, Southern, and modern American literature. He is the author or editor of eight books, including, most recently, biographical studies of contemporary novelists Clarence Major and John Edgar Wideman.

Rikki Ducornet is an essayist, poet, illustrator, and author of the novels *The Jade Cabinet*, *The Fountains of Neptune*, *The Stain*, *The Fan-Maker's Inquisition*, *Phosphor in Dreamland*, *Gazelle*, and *Entering Fire*. Her latest novel, *Brightfellow*, will be published in 2016.

Douglas Field is lecturer in 20th century American Literature at the University of Manchester. He is the author of *All Those Strangers: The Art and Lives of James Baldwin* (2015) and is a regular contributor to the *Times Literary Supplement*. He is currently curating an exhibition of Jeff Nuttall's archive at the John Rylands Library, Manchester.

Thomas Filbin is a book critic whose work has appeared in the *New York Times Book Review*, *The Hudson Review*, and *The Virginia Quarterly Review*. He teaches writing at Suffolk University in Boston.

Monika Fludernik is Professor of English Literature at the University of

Freiburg, Germany. Her major fields of interest include narratology, postcolonial studies, 'Law and Literature', and eighteenth-century aesthetics. She is the author of *The Fictions of Language and the Languages of Fiction* (1993), the award-winning *Towards a 'Natural' Narratology* (1996), *An Introduction to Narratology* (2009) as well as *Echoes and Mirrorings: Gabriel Josipovici's Creative Oeuvre* (2000). Fludernik has edited and co-edited several volumes of essays, including *Diaspora and Multiculturalism: Common Traditions and New Developments* (2003) and *Beyond Cognitive Metaphor Theory: Perspectives on Literary Metaphor* (2011). She has is just completing a study of prison settings and prison metaphors in English literature.

G.N. Forester is something of a nomad and may be based at any one time in Asia, Europe, or the Pacific. Forester currently works as an academic researcher when not writing or editing, and has been known to adopt multiple monikas as a means to obfuscate identification, typical of a paranoid personality.

Michael Freeman was taught how to read by Empson at Sheffield, then tried teaching in schools, teacher-training and the WEA while later an editor at Carcanet and freelance, but remaining—for Brooke-Rose's wry approval—an unreconstructed Northern socialism.

Stephanie Jane Jones is a part-time tutor in the department of English and Creative Writing at Aberystwyth University. She has recently completed a PhD study in the experimental novels of Christine Brooke-Rose and is the co-founder of The Christine Brooke-Rose Society.

James Langdon is an independent graphic designer. He is one of six directors of the artist-run gallery Eastside Projects in Birmingham, UK; and founder of the itinerant School for Design Fiction. In 2012 he received the Inform International Award for Conceptual Design, presented by Galerie für Zeitgenössische Kunst, Leipzig, Germany.

Steven Moore was Managing Editor of Dalkey Archive Press/*Review of Contemporary Fiction* from 1988 to 1996. He is also a literary scholar who has written extensively on William Gaddis and other modern American novelists, as well as on the history of the novel.

M.J. Nicholls is a writer and editor from Glasgow. His comic novel *The House of Writers* will be published in 2016.

Doug Nufer is the author of seven novels and three poetry books. His most recent books are *Lifeline Rule* (Spuyten Duyvil, 2015), *Lounge Acts* (Insert Blanc, 2013), and *By Kelman Out of Pessoa* (Les Figues, 2011). He often performs solo, with other writers, and with musicians or dancers. He runs a wine shop in Seattle.

Garland Osprey is an independently wealthy man of leisure. He is currently co-directing a privately financed production of *Krapp's Last Tape* to be performed at Falkirk Community Centre. His book reviews appear in this book.

Ronald Sukenick (1932-2004) was an essayist, academic, co-founder of the innovative American press Fiction Collective (FC2), and author of the novels *Up, Out, 98.6, Long Talking Bad Conditions Blues, Blown Away, Mosaic Man, Cows,* and *Last Fall.*

Alexander Theroux is an essayist, poet, and author of the novels *Darconville's Cat, Laura Warholic: The Sexual Intellectual, An Adultery,* and *Three Wogs.*

Nicolas Tredell has interviewed many writers and published widely on novelists such as Martin Amis, Christine Brooke-Rose, David Caute, Joseph Conrad, Charles Dickens, William Faulkner, Scott Fitzgerald, B. S. Johnson, Ann Quin, Simon Raven, David Storey and Colin Wilson. Verbivoracious Press brought out a new edition of his interview collection *Conversations with Critics* in 2015.

John Trefry is a U.S. author and architect living in Lawrence, Kansas. His text-based work includes a novel *Plats,* a capricious internet usurping collage *Thy Decay Thou Seest By Thy Desire*, and the forthcoming novel *Apparitions of the Living.* One partner, three cats, four chickens.

Dana A. Williams is Professor and Chair of English at Howard University and DA specialist in contemporary African American Literature. In addition to an annotated bibliography, *Contemporary African American Female Playwrights: An Annotated Bibliography* (Greenwood 1999), she has co-edited *August Wilson and Black Aesthetics* (Palgrave-MacMillan, 2004) with Sandra G. Shannon, edited *African American Humor, Irony, and Satire: Ishmael Reed, Satirically Speaking* (Cambridge Scholars, 2007), *Conversations with Leon Forrest* (UP of Mississippi, 2007), and *Contemporary African American Fiction: New Critical Essays* (Ohio State UP, 2009). She is also the author of the first and only book-length study on *Leon Forrest, In the Light of Likeness—Transformed: The Literary Art of Leon Forrest* (Ohio State UP, 2005). She is the past president of the Association of the Departments of English Executive Committee, Chair of the Black American Literature and Culture Forum for the Modern Languages Association, and President of the College Language Association—the oldest and largest professional organization for faculty of color who teach languages and literatures.